ISSUE 13, OCTOBER 2021

AUSTRALIAN FOREIGN AFFAIRS

Contributors

Dennis Altman is a professorial fellow in the Institute for Human Security at La Trobe University.

Aarti Betigeri is a journalist who writes regularly on South Asian issues.

Elizabeth Buchanan is a lecturer in strategic studies at Deakin University and a fellow of the Modern War Institute at West Point Military Academy.

James Curran is a professor of history at the University of Sydney.

Donald Greenlees is an award-winning journalist and a senior adviser at Asialink, the University of Melbourne.

Jane Perlez is a former Beijing bureau chief for *The New York Times* and the anchor for an upcoming podcast on Nixon's 1972 trip to China.

Snigdha Poonam is a journalist based in New Delhi.

Harsh V. Pant is Head of Strategic Studies at the Observer Research Foundation in New Delhi and a professor of international relations at King's College London.

Michael Wesley is Deputy Vice-Chancellor International at the University of Melbourne.

Australian Foreign Affairs is published three times a year by Schwartz Books Pty Ltd. Publisher: Morry Schwartz. ISBN 978-1-76064-2129 ISSN 2208-5912 ALL RIGHTS RESERVED. No part of this publication may be reproduced, stored in a retrieval system, or transmitted in any form by any means, electronic, mechanical, photocopying, recording or otherwise, without the prior consent of the publishers. Essays, reviews and correspondence © retained by the authors. Subscriptions – 1 year print & digital auto-renew (3 issues): $49.99 within Australia incl. GST. 1 year print and digital subscription (3 issues): $59.99 within Australia incl. GST. 2 year print & digital (6 issues): $114.99 within Australia incl. GST. 1 year digital only auto-renew: $29.99. Payment may be made by MasterCard, Visa or Amex, or by cheque made out to Schwartz Books Pty Ltd. Payment includes postage and handling. To subscribe, fill out the form inside this issue, subscribe online at www.australianforeignaffairs.com, email subscribe@australianforeignaffairs.com or phone 1800 077 514 / 61 3 9486 0288. Correspondence should be addressed to: The Editor, Australian Foreign Affairs, Level 1, 221 Drummond Street, Carlton VIC 3053 Australia Phone: 61 3 9486 0288 / Fax: 61 3 9486 0244 Email: enquiries@australianforeignaffairs.com Editor: Jonathan Pearlman. Deputy Editor: Julia Carlomagno. Associate Editor: Chris Feik. Consulting Editor: Allan Gyngell. Digital Editor and Marketing: Amy Rudder. Editorial Intern: Lachlan McIntosh. Management: Elisabeth Young. Subscriptions: Iryna Byelyayeva and Sam Perazzo. Publicity: Anna Lensky. Design: Peter Long. Production Coordination and Typesetting: Tristan Main. Cover photographs by Getty Images / *Hindustan Times*. Printed in Australia by McPherson's Printing Group.

Editor's Note

INDIA RISING?

In 2014, Narendra Modi visited Australia, marking the first visit by an Indian prime minister in twenty-eight years. The reception was rapturous. Tony Abbott, Australia's prime minister, hugged Modi – three times – and described him as "almost a brother". In Sydney, the Indian leader addressed a stadium packed with 16,000 people, who chanted "Modi, Modi, Modi" as the dignitaries onstage excitedly took photos of him on their phones.

A new era seemed to have arrived, in which Australia and India would finally make good on the relationship, which appeared to hold so much promise – two democracies, a shared colonial heritage, bookends of the Indian Ocean – but had remained perennially unfulfilled. Abbott promised a free trade deal within a year. Modi promised that Australia would not have to wait so long for the next visit by an Indian leader.

Seven years later, there is no free trade deal. Modi has no plans to revisit. Other promises, such as enabling a steady supply of Australian uranium to India, appear to have been waylaid or forgotten.

It would be easy, then, to reach a familiar conclusion: that India and Australia can never deliver on the hype; that the relationship is defined by their differences. India, for instance, favours foreign policy non-alignment and autonomy, whereas Australia celebrates its alliance with the United States. Neither government has been able to boost the paltry two-way flows of trade and investment.

But the relationship is changing. Last October, India invited Australia to join the annual Malabar naval exercise, which also involves the United States and Japan. Australia participated again in 2021. These exercises followed the revival of the Quadrilateral Security Dialogue, a grouping that includes India, Australia, the United States and Japan. In March, Joe Biden hosted a summit of the leaders of the Quad, solidifying its status.

This growing security relationship between Australia and India reflects their common anxieties about the threat posed by a rising China. In recent years, both have clashed with Beijing: Australia has been targeted by Chinese economic sanctions, and India has been involved in deadly fighting with China along their contested Himalayan border. India and Australia share a heritage, but they now also – more significantly – share a rival.

The other key change, evident from the packed stadium in 2014, is that Australia's Indian-born population is booming. Indian-born Australians make up 3 per cent of the population, a higher proportion than those born in China. Australia's growing and diverse Indian diaspora community should help it to boost trade and engagement with India; it should also help Australian policymakers, businesses and diplomats to overcome some of the misunderstandings that have impeded ties in the past.

Obstacles remain. India is one of the world's most protectionist countries, it is wary of security alliances and its largest military supplier is Russia. Modi is a staunch Hindu nationalist who – according to a 2021 report by Washington-based think tank Freedom House – has undermined civil liberties and "abandoned [India's] potential to serve as a global democratic leader". As former Australian prime minister Malcolm Turnbull told an event at La Trobe University in August: "The idea that you can delete China, insert India, is just nonsense."

Yet as Asia's power balance changes, there is a genuine opportunity to finally create a close and meaningful India–Australia partnership. To seize on this potential, Australia will finally need to understand the limitations of the relationship, and find ways to overcome them.

Jonathan Pearlman

PIVOT TO INDIA

Our next great
and powerful friend?

Michael Wesley

In the stifling mid-afternoon heat near the remote town of Pokhran, in the Rajasthani desert, on 11 May 1998, India detonated one fusion-based and two fission-based nuclear warheads. Two days later, it detonated two more fission-based warheads.

Prime Minister Atal Bihari Vajpayee announced India's arrival as a nuclear power. It had planned and executed the tests, he said, to gather data for computer simulations, which would allow India to develop its nuclear capacities without the need for further tests. And it had taken the world by surprise: despite intensive US monitoring of the site, no one outside a small coterie of Indian officials had any idea of the scale, sophistication or imminence of the tests.

Australia's response was swift and damning. Minister for Foreign Affairs Alexander Downer called the tests "outrageous acts" and Prime Minister John Howard referred to them as a "grotesque status symbol".

Canberra suspended ministerial contacts, defence cooperation and non-humanitarian aid to New Delhi. While other nations also condemned India's tests, and Australia took even harsher measures against Pakistan when it carried out its own nuclear tests a fortnight later, New Delhi took particular exception to Australia's reaction. It enacted retaliatory measures and heaped derision on Australia's hypocrisy. Only a country entirely dependent on another's nuclear umbrella for its own defence could act holier-than-thou towards a country in a tough neighbourhood needing to look to its own means, argued Indian diplomats. The sniping continued in the following months.

The 1998 Pokhran tests represent the nadir of Australia's relationship with India. Both sides drew on decades of misunderstandings and irritations. For Australian officials, the tests showcased India's tendency to buck international consensus and to hide self-interest behind condescending moral principle. For Indians, Australia's hectoring arose from a privileged, white, probably racist attitude, talking down to others while cowering under America's strategic skirts.

But Pokhran also marks a turning point in Australia–India relations. Two years later Howard visited India, the first Australian prime minister to have done so since 1989. The Indian defence secretary visited Australia the same year, inaugurating a dialogue that has deepened ever since. Bilateral trade began to expand quickly, leaping from $3 billion in 2000 to more than AU$20 billion a decade later. No longer is it the case that, as foreign policy specialist Allan Gyngell once quipped, "every Australian government discovers India once, and then promptly forgets about it". India has emerged as a bipartisan foreign policy priority for Australia. India, as well, has begun to take its relations with Australia seriously.

Measures of mutual regard and collaboration have continued to proliferate. In June 2020, prime ministers Scott Morrison and Narendra Modi signed a Comprehensive Strategic Partnership, with annual 2+2 Foreign and Defence Ministerial Consultations (opportunities for discussion reserved by each for its most important relationships). The partnership sets out an ambitious agenda of collaboration on science, technology, defence, counterterrorism, regional diplomacy, innovation, agriculture, water, governance, education, tourism and culture. Talks on a free trade agreement inch forward, and each nation has produced a strategy for increasing economic engagement with the other. They are enthusiastic participants in the Quadrilateral Security Dialogue (the Quad), which includes Japan and the United States and is meeting increasingly at steadily more senior levels.

As Australia's relationship with China has soured, probably irretrievably, India has emerged as the great new hope across the political spectrum and through diverse sectors of the economy and society. In seeking to diversify away from one big developing market, businesses have begun to focus on the only other with a scale and dynamism that comes close to China's. And as Australia views China in increasingly threatening terms, it finds ever more reasons to seek common cause with a fellow democracy, a significant and growing military power with its own conflictual relationship with Beijing. With America's lurch towards Trumpism leading to nervousness about US power and commitment, even to close allies – a fear that persists with Biden in the White House – will India emerge as a new "great and powerful friend" for Australia?

That phrase, coined by Menzies, has become a leitmotif in Australian foreign policy because it describes an essential truth: Australia relies on special relationships with great powers for its security. As Sir Robert put it pithily in a speech before the 1958 election, "The dominant element in our foreign policy is, of course, to maintain friendly relations; to be good neighbours; to have powerful friends. Why powerful friends? Does anybody suppose that we could in our own strength defend ourselves against a major aggressor?"

As Australia's relationship with China has soured ... India has emerged as the great new hope

Australia, it seems, has started to envisage a substantial role for India in its strategic future. But it is not clear exactly what this role will look like. Nor is it clear that India is prepared to play the function Australia may want it to. As China becomes more assertive, Canberra must think hard about how India may or may not complement its other important relationships in ensuring a favourable regional order in the decades ahead. This will involve thinking about Australia's needs, as well as pondering how great, how powerful and how friendly India will be.

The roots of estrangement

The relationship between Australia and independent India was born troubled. By 1947 Australia had become accustomed to holding a privileged position within the British Empire, as a dominion with a full panoply of prerogatives and expectations. In 1906 Alfred Deakin, Australia's prime minister, wrote in the London *Morning Post* that "the British Empire, though united in the whole, is, nevertheless, divided broadly into two parts, one occupied wholly or mainly by a white ruling race, the other occupied by coloured races, who are ruled. Australia and New Zealand are determined to keep their place in the first class." As India struggled for independence and for recognition of the major contribution it had made to the Empire during two world wars, Australia's leaders were unsympathetic to its efforts to be granted entry to the small club of privileged dominions. Even after Indian independence in 1947, the inner circle persisted: the white dominions – Australia, Canada, South Africa and New Zealand – made sure that Commonwealth meetings reserved them a space for confidential talks with the British.

Little wonder, then, that there was scant warmth for Australia in India's new government. India's first prime minister, Jawaharlal Nehru, and Australia's prime minister, Robert Menzies, treated each other with icy civility in public; in private, Menzies was as dismissive of India's stance of non-alignment as Nehru was of Australia's perceived subordination to the British and the Americans. The White Australia policy established a lasting view of Australia as a racist society, akin to South Africa, in the minds of an Indian elite deeply indignant at the racist condescension of the British Raj. At a personal level, when they met at universities, sporting contests and international meetings, Indians and Australians more often than not rubbed each other the wrong way. Indians found Australians loud, brash and uncultured; Australians found Indians haughty, prickly and judgemental.

Apart from shared membership in the Commonwealth and a mutual love of cricket, there seemed to be little that brought India and Australia together. India's championing of the Non-Aligned Movement and pan-Asianism, and initial closeness to Mao's China and Sukarno's Indonesia, raised Australian fears about being surrounded by militant nationalist independent states leaning towards socialism. India was adamantly opposed to Australia's approach to Asia, which centred on expanding the American alliance system and fighting expeditionary wars to stop the spread of communism.

Geopolitically, India and Australia also occupied different universes. India had been divided against its will at independence, and within twenty years of self-rule had suffered major attacks from its two most powerful neighbours, Pakistan and China. There was no superpower ally that it could or would turn to for help; its relationship with the Soviet Union from the late 1960s was largely transactional. India continues even today to be beset by internal secessionism and irridentist claims along its major land borders. Its strategic attention is focused northwards, towards its unremittingly hostile neighbours: Pakistan in the west and China in the east. The partnership between Beijing and Islamabad means that India has long faced the German dilemma: the possibility of a two-front war against capable and coordinated enemies.

In almost perfect contrast, Australia is an island with no territorial disputes or significant powerful neighbours. To assuage its central anxiety – that it has too few people to defend such a large landmass – it has formed close alliances with culturally and ideologically congruent major powers. American dominance in the Pacific has freed Australia to concentrate on developing trade and investment links with the booming economies of Pacific Asia, and on building institutions to solidify regional relations and prosperity. Just as India's strategic gaze has traditionally been to the north, away from Australia, Australia's gaze was to the north and east, away from India. In the 1980s, when laying out its grand scheme for the Asia-Pacific Economic Cooperation (APEC) forum, an institution that would unite Australia and Asia in shared security and prosperity, Canberra was adamantly opposed to including India.

The subcontinent rotates

The abrupt end to the Cold War left India contemplating the wisdom of its post-independence foreign and economic policies. The Gandhian struggle against imperialism had left a compelling imprint on Nehru. He determined that India would not engage in the tawdry power politics of the postwar world. It would subvert the very idea of the great power, which had led to colonialism and caused so much suffering; it would become the antithesis of a power obsessed by might, coercion and exploitation. India would cleave to its own development path, becoming self-reliant and responsive only to its own economic dictates, and it would lead by example.

India's humiliation by China in the 1962 border war carried the bitter lesson that military strength was necessary for self-preservation against great powers unmoved by moral appeals. With the United States increasingly unsympathetic – Washington was inclined to back Pakistan and looking to normalise its relations with China – India began to gravitate towards the Soviet Union. It would never be an ideological alignment, but the Soviet relationship allowed the rapid development of India's military power, enabling its defeat of Pakistan in the war of 1971. China's nuclear tests in 1964 prompted the acceleration of India's own nuclear program, leading to an initial test in 1974. Military interventions in the Maldives and Sri Lanka in the 1980s marked a further divergence from the Nehruvian roots of Indian foreign policy.

> India's future as a great power would not involve land, but sea

The collapse of the Soviet Union in 1991 deprived India of both its major backer and the bipolar world order that had made non-alignment possible. That year also saw India plunge into the most serious economic crisis it has ever faced: a deficit in its balance of payments (its monetary transactions with the rest of the world), combined with a sudden currency depreciation and high government debt, left the country unable to finance its import needs at a time when the Gulf War had sent oil prices through the roof. The Nehruvian development strategy of import substitution and state-led industrialisation was widely blamed and, following an International Monetary Fund bailout, a program of economic liberalisation was adopted. India's economic growth began to accelerate.

The 1990s also saw the beginning of the end of the Congress Party's dominance of national politics. The assassination of Prime Minister Rajiv Gandhi in 1991 left Congress without a natural leader, and the Bharatiya Janata Party (BJP) came to power in 1998. The BJP had emerged as a confluence of movements opposed to the Gandhi–Nehru vision of India, particularly to Congress's commitment to secularism, which critics saw as neglecting the Hindu majority to chase the votes of minorities. It was the BJP that took the step over the nuclear threshold. Its determined response to Pakistani infiltration over the Line of Control in the Kargil sector of Kashmir in 1999 led to an outpouring of Indian patriotism and support for muscular self-defence. Writers advocating the placement of realpolitik at the centre of Indian foreign policy, and the need to make good on its great-power potential, became more prominent in the public debate.

But perhaps the most significant achievement of the BJP government of Atal Bihari Vajpayee between 1998 and 2004 was to draw India into greater alignment with the United States and its key allies. Amid the storm of criticism surrounding the Pokhran nuclear tests, earlier Indian governments would likely have withdrawn into wounded self-righteousness. Instead, Vajpayee placed former finance minister Jaswant Singh in charge of easing India's diplomatic isolation by negotiating directly with the United States to improve relations. Working feverishly with Strobe Talbott, a lion of American diplomacy, Singh, soon to be elevated to Minister for External Affairs, achieved a remarkable turnaround in ties with the United States and its allies. By March 2000, US president Bill Clinton stood in India's parliament and spoke of a partnership between India and the United States on free trade, democracy and nuclear non-proliferation.

The BJP lost the 2004 elections and Congress returned to power, but India had crossed a threshold. The party of Gandhi and Nehru maintained and developed India's civilian and military nuclear capabilities, signing a nuclear partnership with the United States and ending India's isolation from key non-proliferation and uranium supply institutions. Soviet-inspired military doctrine was abandoned and India embarked on modernising its armed forces. Reforms saw its economy grow; trade and foreign investment rose. Once prickly, contrarian and slow-moving, India had started to look much more like a familiar great power.

The emergence of India as a maritime power was even more momentous than its crossing of the nuclear rubicon. After independence, India viewed its main threats as coming from the north and west. From the Sino–Indian War of 1962 on, India invested heavily in its army and air force, largely to the neglect of its navy. The Indian navy was starved of resources, prestige and strategic rationale – until 1971, when the Nixon administration positioned an aircraft carrier battlegroup in the Bay of Bengal during the Indo–Pakistani War as a direct threat to India. It was a pointless gesture that had no effect on the war's outcome, but India saw it as a humiliating lesson about the need for naval power.

India's naval build-up began in the mid-1970s and gained real momentum in the 1990s. In the meantime, Indian strategists rediscovered the significance of the Indian Ocean. London had sought to protect Britain's Indian empire by turning the Indian Ocean into a British lake, controlling its points of entry and keeping all hostile interests out. India's long eastern and western coastlines overlooked three of the world's most important maritime thoroughfares: the Malacca Strait, the entrance to the Gulf and the entrance to the Suez Canal. No other existing or emerging naval powers had significant bases in or near the Indian Ocean. India's future as a great power would not involve land, but sea.

The elephant in the room

India's emergence as a naval power came at a key moment in global power politics. As the big economies of North-East Asia industrialised, they became increasingly dependent on energy supplies from the Gulf. The Indian Ocean was a crucial thoroughfare – and the Indian subcontinent projects like the tip of a spear across that thoroughfare. The Indian navy sits within striking distance of the two major choke points in the world's energy superhighway: the entrance to the Gulf and the entrance to the Malacca Strait.

This development, more than any other, explains the remarkable reorientation in the West's attitudes towards India. By 2010 it had become clear that China's power and ambition had gained a momentum of their own, unbound by considerations of restraint or reassurance.

Integration into the global economy and regional institutions had only emboldened Beijing. China's list of confrontations was lengthening, the abrasiveness of its statecraft had become more overt and its willingness to revert to unorthodox methods of coercion was more apparent.

One of China's most serious strategic liabilities continues to be its dependence on energy from the Gulf. This has given India an outsize advantage over its long-time antagonist, even while its economy and military spending are dwarfed by China's. The interruption of energy flows across the Indian Ocean for even a comparatively short period could bring the Chinese economy to a shuddering halt and deprive its armed forces of significant capabilities to fight a conventional conflict; India has no strategic vulnerability to China of corresponding significance. This has caused Beijing to turn its attention to developing its own maritime power in the Indian Ocean.

The United States got there before Australia, realising India's potential as it watched China

As the United States and its allies cast around for any opportunity to place limits on Beijing's capabilities and ambitions, India's maritime position and potential loom large. Following Clinton's speech to the Indian parliament in 2000, his successors Bush, Obama and Trump all visited India, and all vowed to strengthen the relationship in order to help India emerge as a great power. More American presidents have visited India in the last twenty years than in the preceding half-century. Japan, once dismissive of and distant towards India, has embarked on a concerted effort to engage with it economically, technologically and militarily. South Korea is now a major investor in the Indian economy. Not since the emergence of the United States as a great power at the end of the nineteenth century has a rising power been attended to by so many well-wishers.

Australia discovers its other coast

For most of its post-1788 history, Australia has ignored the Indian Ocean. Unlike the Pacific, the Indian has no major island chains. Its one major littoral economy, India, was a British colony, and once independent, remained closed and inward-looking. Although from the opening of the Suez Canal in 1869 Australia became heavily dependent on shipping across the Indian Ocean, there was little cause for anxiety while the British navy maintained it as a British lake. Australian and British ships fought several skirmishes in the Indian Ocean during the world wars, but conflict was never serious enough to elevate its western approaches from the status, in Australia's strategic imagination, of a geopolitical dead zone.

Instead, Australia was fixated on its Pacific approaches. Its northern and eastern shores were girdled with archipelagoes that could – and did – become forward bases for hostile powers. The Pacific was bordered by major powers, both imperial and Asian. It was the site of incessant battles, and of the world's first war fought with naval and air forces across thousands of kilometres of ocean and islands. It was here that communism seemed most virulently on the march. And it was the rapid development of the Pacific's major economies that produced a surge in demand for Australia's energy, minerals and food at a time when the British economy was turning towards Europe.

If the Pacific was Australia's source of strategic anxiety, US power and regional institutions were its fount of reassurance. The end of the Cold War saw Canberra invest heavily in both; a deepened alliance would anchor US power more firmly in the Pacific, while strong institutions such as APEC would integrate China into a prosperous, liberal regional order. But the scale of China's ambitions and the dynamism of the region's economies soon posed questions about the adequacy of US power and regional institutions, as well as about treating the Pacific as a separate region of development and strategy. Ambitions and appetites overspilled the Pacific, most significantly into Australia's northwestern oceanic approaches. Canberra quietly jettisoned the Asia-Pacific as its regional imaginary and began to speak of the Indo-Pacific. Then Japanese prime minister Shinzō Abe spoke of the "confluence" of the Indian and Pacific oceans. The United States renamed its Pacific Command the Indo-Pacific Command.

Australia has grappled with how to make sense of its Indian Ocean frontier. Its enthusiastic championing of an Indian Ocean Rim Association has delivered scant results. Its leaders and strategists debate where the Indian Ocean region ends – is it at the Indo-Pakistani border, the Gulf, the east coast of Africa? The one thing all agree on is the pivotal role India will play in securing a favourable order in the Indo-Pacific's western reaches. What is yet to be seen is what that role will look like.

Great-power dreaming

Australia's foreign policy persona has been shaped by close partnerships with culturally similar great powers. Unlike other postcolonial states, it has never regarded this dependence as a liability or a source of shame. Its foreign policy has tended to be "heliocentric" – the major elements of its statecraft are shaped by its commitment to a single major ally. It dreads the weakening of its alliance relationship. The option of abandoning or endangering the alliance for other goals (as New Zealand did with its nuclear-free policy) has never moved beyond the straw-man stage of policy discussion in Canberra.

Heliocentrism has enshrined a presidential element to policy formation, with the prime minister taking personal charge of relations with the major ally. It has also resulted in Australia looking at the world from the same perspective as a global power, rather than as an isolated country with limited capabilities. Our institutions of state have always hummed with discussion of international power alignments and preoccupations with events a long way from our shores. As a consequence, we have developed an expectation of having a major voice in global councils and a willingness to undertake expeditionary military ventures. Few other countries of Australia's size exhibit these expectations and tendencies.

Heliocentrism also makes Australia prone to a fascination with rising powers. An intense strand of admiration for the United States arose in the 1860s, long before the ANZUS Treaty was signed in 1951. Japan's defeat of Russia in 1905 brought both respect and alarm, which steadily intensified through the first half of the twentieth century. Admiration for Japan's rapid industrial rise after World War II underpinned Australia's swift reconciliation with its former adversary. And only a heliocentric perspective can explain the exuberant engagement with China after 1972, followed by a collapse into paranoid pessimism in the past decade.

Australia's heliocentric sensitivities have underpinned its changing perspective on India. While New Delhi embarked on its anti–great power Nehruvian foreign policy, Canberra struggled to fit this policy alignment into its global outlook. An unwillingness to rise to conventional power drew Australia's contempt; it was interpreted as an inability to act with determination

A more antagonistic China makes India a more compelling partner

on the world stage. This deep misconception motivated Howard's and Downer's disparaging responses to India's 1998 nuclear tests. Their comments were appropriate to untrustworthy pretenders such as Pakistan or North Korea, rather than to a rising power enhancing its capabilities.

The United States got there before Australia, realising India's potential as it watched China's trajectory. It helped that after 1998, India started to look more like a conventional great power. A cohort of Asian states respected by Australia – Singapore, Japan, South Korea, Vietnam – had also begun publicly factoring India into the evolving regional order. As these nations – along with European powers such as Britain and France – looked favourably on India's ambitions to become the paramount naval power in the Indian Ocean, so Australian policy-makers began to see India through others' eyes.

Australia brings two major assets to building its relationship with India. One is its close relationship with the United States – an irony given that this intimacy once made Indians dismissive of Australia's foreign policy independence. Now India sees Australia as an anchor that grounds the stabilising ship of the United States in Indo-Pacific waters. While India would never contemplate allowing US destroyers regular access to its naval bases, it is comfortable with Australian bases providing support to US fleets. The other asset is the Australian navy, the second-most powerful of any Indian Ocean littoral state. That Australia accepts a legitimate role for the Indian navy in the Indian Ocean makes it easier for other significant littoral states, such as Indonesia and Malaysia, to accept it also.

The rapid souring of Australia's relationship with China has added further momentum to Indo–Australian ties. A more antagonistic China makes India a more compelling partner. And no Indo-Pacific capital would have been more gratified than New Delhi at Canberra's newly confrontational attitude towards Beijing. Australia, the United States and Japan are now aligned with India's sense of Indo-Pacific power relations, as shown by consequential meetings of the Quad and the regularity with which the naval forces of the four countries train with one another.

An unfamiliar partner

The prevailing view in Australia, on all sides of politics, is that India is a natural geopolitical partner. Significant commonalities help: both nations are democracies; the growth of the Indian diaspora in Australia has fostered greater cultural understanding; and the Indian cricket team now plays with the sort of ruthless competitiveness that once defined Australian cricketers. With the controversy over the Adani mine, an Indian conglomerate has entered the public consciousness – perhaps the harbinger of the next wave of Asian investment after those from Japan and China. India now has a natural role in global forums such as the G20 and is widely seen as a future major power. And, aside from China and Pakistan, it has relatively benign relations with its neighbours. Its willingness to settle maritime disputes in the Bay of Bengal consensually stands in stark contrast to China's behaviour in the South China Sea.

Personal relationships have helped. Indian prime minister Narendra Modi has developed a warm rapport with a succession of Australian counterparts of differing personalities: Tony Abbott, Malcolm Turnbull and Scott Morrison. Beyond Australia, Modi charmed Shinzō Abe and Donald Trump. There are elements of his populist political style and can-do approach to governance that appeal to conservative leaders, who are more likely to overlook his government's chauvinistic approach to communal relations at home.

But there are challenges for Australia in India's growing role in the Indo-Pacific. Those in Canberra who expect India to rise to power on the steep trajectory sketched by Japan and China will be disappointed. As a former Australian high commissioner to New Delhi, Peter Varghese, has observed, India will develop according to its own timetable. Its economic development will lag its military capabilities, just as its economic integration with Australia, Japan and other regional economies will lag its strategic alignment with the Quad.

India certainly looks more like a conventional great power now than in the past, but it will never be a great power of the sort that Australia has become familiar with. Britain, the United States, imperial Japan and communist China have all been effective at concentrating and deploying power. India, and probably later Indonesia, will be a different proposition. Vast internal diversity and the absence of what Russians refer to as a "power vertical" – a clear and authoritative hierarchy of control over society and economy – will always make the power India can wield outside its borders disproportionate to its size.

These attributes will be disorienting for Australia and will test its commitment to building a partnership. But the emergence of India as a great power reveals an even more profoundly disruptive consequence for Australia. The US investment in a relationship with India signals an admission that America has neither the capacity nor the stomach to face down China alone. Washington has ceded its pre-eminence in the Pacific to an order in which China and the United States become two among a series of great powers – including Indonesia and Japan – seeking to prevent any single state from dominating the region.

This represents a deep challenge to Australia's heliocentric foreign policy, which stretches back to 1788. For the first time, there will be no single great power that will be the guarantor of Australia's security or the centre of gravity for its statecraft. Australia will have to adapt to a multipolar regional order – perhaps the greatest challenge its institutions and policymaking processes have ever faced.

The rise of India in a multipolar Asia confronts Canberra with several imperatives. It needs to recognise India's role as a great power irrespective of the US–India relationship, which will fluctuate as the power balance in Asia shifts. Canberra should build ties with New Delhi that are decoupled from the vicissitudes of great-power positioning. Nor should Australia

Nor should Australia expect the Quad to guarantee its relationship with India

expect the Quad – or any other multilateral organisation – to guarantee its relationship with India.

Canberra needs to jettison the view that India's democracy will automatically ensure some sort of permanent alignment with other democratic states. Great powers, whatever their politics, are selfish, solipsistic and capricious. Other states must learn to live with them on these terms. As we have long known in regard to Indonesia, there will be occasions in which the United States prioritises its relationship with India over its relationship with Australia. Our heliocentric perspective is a liability in a multipolar world; only by negotiating and balancing relationships with the several poles can we protect our interests.

Finally, the security of the Indian Ocean must remain an abiding preoccupation. Given that Australia has the second-strongest navy of any littoral state, it should work with India to engage other states in efforts to ensure stability there. Cooperation on maritime security and freedom of passage in our shared waters – not democracy, cricket or the Commonwealth – is where the most powerful alignment between our two nations truly lies. ■

NEW WAVE

Australia's nation-changing Indian diaspora

Aarti Betigeri

Almost a decade ago, Melbourne artist Sapna Chandu wondered why chai – proper Indian-style masala chai – was nowhere to be found in Australian cafes, yet the dialled-down Western version, chai latte, was everywhere. It led her to conceptualise a world where India had overtaken Australia and had staged a cultural coup.

The installation, *Kwality Chai*, which was presented at the 2014 Melbourne Fringe Festival, was an immersive experience where viewers entered a parallel reality, set forty years after India had successfully staged a Y2K IT takeover of Australia and now ruled as a colonial power. In this imagined future, there was still a love of caffeine in Melbourne, but it was masala chai that everyone queued for. Inside the *Kwality Chai* space, viewers would order chai from someone speaking with an Indian lilt and using hybrid Anglo-Indian phrases, set against an aural landscape featuring the tooting horns of an Indian street. They would drink the tea while listening to a radio featuring R&B and old Bollywood, interspersed with news bulletins discussing events such as, say, an auto rickshaw colliding with a tram, or the Australian prime minister, J.J. Vijayalakshmi, considering extending Indian laws into its new colony. They could pick up a newspaper and read about the challenge to beef-eating laws. What began as an exploration of cultural appropriation ended as one of cultural imperialism – but in this case, in reverse to the usual way it happens.

Kwality Chai came to mind the minute I started thinking critically about the Indian diaspora in Australia and about how a future Australia might look as growing numbers of Indians settle here. Usually, Australian art takes a Western-centred approach to India, whether it is about Indian culture, or the experiences of a Westerner in India, or an Indian's struggles to fit into Australia. But this was the first time an artist – a second-generation Indian Australian – had centred the Indians, the migrants, putting them in the driver's seat of culture.

It was prescient then, and it is prescient now, in 2021, as it becomes clear that migration from India will continue to grow, and the group will help power Australia's economic growth. And this demographic change is occurring just as a bolder India is set to play a larger role in Asia and in Australia's approach to the region. As the Indian diaspora in Australia becomes larger, stronger and more prominent, it is an opportune time to take a closer look at its shape and characteristics.

Early connections

Australia and India were once connected via land, both part of Gond-wanaland, a supercontinent that existed until about 180 million years ago. There is some evidence of ancient links between Australia and India – a 1999 study asserts a maternal genetic connection between the two countries, and a 2013 study of Indigenous Australian DNA suggests there might have been migration from India about 4000 years ago. Even disbelievers cannot fail to notice some pockets of similarity, such as the resemblance between India's Gond art and Indigenous dot painting, or that dingoes look uncannily like Indian street dogs.

Fast-forward to the 1800s, and South Asians were moving to Australia, first as labour for the British but later as camel drivers – and, importantly, camel owners. The cameleers are usually referred to as Afghans, but there is evidence that they came from a broad stretch spanning the subcontinent, from modern-day Afghanistan and Pakistan, across northern India, to Bengal. Samia Khatun's 2019 book *Australianama* tells of a nineteenth-century Bengali-language book of songs and stories that was discovered in the Broken Hill mosque, indicating that Bengalis were present in Australia at that time. Back then, Indians and Afghans came to Australia to seek work as cameleers or in other occupations often not as a permanent migration, but rather to make money and have some life experiences – much like, it must be said, every backpacker and global nomad today.

In the decades that followed, Indians kept coming, some to work the goldfields, or in sugar and banana plantations, or as hawkers. One,

Siva Singh, hawked groceries and goods around farms in the Benalla region of Victoria in the early 1900s. According to the Australian Indian Historical Society, Singh was struck off the electoral rolls in 1915 in line with the White Australia policy's limits on who was recognised as Australian, but he successfully lobbied to be restored, taking his fight to the High Court. He was one of thousands of Indian hawkers at the time, some of whom amassed fortunes and built solid links with their local communities. Benalla now features a memorial to Siva Singh.

By the time of Federation, the Indian population had reached around 7600 people. But the inflow stopped once Australia's erstwhile rulers – and voters – decided that they wanted to keep the population lily-white – in contrast to the black lie that modern Australia was founded upon.

The first modern wave

The White Australia policy came to a definitive end in 1973 under Gough Whitlam, after the Holt government had, seven years earlier, started moving away from the controversial policy to account for a potential migrant's qualifications and skills, and not their race. Indians and Asians and people of other nationalities had already begun arriving under the Colombo Plan, which ushered in a smattering of students in the 1950s.

An early scholar who came to Australia was Jayant Bapat, now an adjunct research professor at the Monash Asia Institute at Melbourne's Monash University. He arrived in 1965 after completing a master's degree in organic chemistry in India and receiving a scholarship to study further at Monash. Before he departed, friends advised him to start learning German; Indians had barely heard of Australia. When he arrived, the White Australia policy was still in effect, but he recalls having little problem with racism or hostility: "because there were so few Indians, we were a novelty".

He describes an Australia at once familiar and unfamiliar: bracingly cold, lonely, no inside toilets, little food he could recognise. The Punjabis he lived with would make an approximation of vegetable curry using Keen's curry powder; he says he grew used to its cardboardy taste. It was six years into his stay before the correct flour to make chapati, the bread that is the mainstay of Indian home cooking, became available, and even then it had to be specially ordered,

Migration patterns led to what is essentially a fragmented community

taking weeks or months to arrive. He also found the Australian accent virtually unintelligible. But overall, he felt welcomed and nurtured, and, despite initially having had no plans to relocate, he decided to stay. Fifty-five years later, he is a highly valued member of the community, and works voluntarily as a pandit, or Hindu priest, officiating at weddings (including mine) and funerals. He writes about the Indian diaspora, migration and Hinduism for the Monash Asia Institute.

My parents, too, were early arrivals: my father in 1968 and my mother in 1971. My father had decided on Australia after looking at the options: he was turned off the United States and the United Kingdom because of the race riots in Detroit and Notting Hill. Australia had its racism enshrined in policy, but at least people weren't whacking one another in the streets, he reasoned. Almost immediately he was offered a job at a hospital in Swan Hill, so left his world behind.

My father came from a small, traditional town in northern Karnataka state, not far from the tourist centre of Hampi, and my mother from a wealthy and progressive family in Mumbai; despite their differences, they flourished in Australia, building a solid social network. There weren't many Indians, so while they made friends with others – mostly other doctors, truth be told – their social connections extended into wider Australian society: to neighbours and the school community.

After a few years of working in hospitals, my father took over a flourishing medical practice in the suburbs and quickly built up a solid roster of patients – some of whom remained on his books for forty years. My mother worked at local schools as a librarian, and for years wore saris to work every day. My father, a lapsed vegetarian, struggled with the food – in particular, the corned beef served at the hospital canteen. But otherwise, they were the very model of the kind of grateful, pliable migrants that Australia loves best: they brought their skills and grit to the new country; they held onto the more palatable parts of their culture but shed other bits; they worked hard to adjust, acclimatise, even assimilate.

There is a saying that Indian migrants like to repeat: Indians, when in a new place, dissolve like sugar in milk, invisible but making everything sweeter. (The story was actually co-opted from the Parsi community, which tells it as part of the tale of its move from Persia to India in the seventh century.) There are large Indian migrant communities in many parts of the world – the United Kingdom, South Africa, East Africa, the Caribbean, Fiji, Guyana, Malaysia, Singapore, the United States, Canada – and all generally find acceptability in their adopted homelands, albeit to varying degrees. Indians tend to be entrepreneurial, opening shops, hotels, restaurants and other businesses, and in many places quickly rise up the socio-economic ranks thanks to their work ethic and zeal. In particular, Indian migrants have found the United States to be a welcoming environment and have achieved great success there. There, they have a median income double that of the wider population and have

India accounts for the largest number of new Australian citizens

managed to break through the bamboo ceilings that exist even in the most exclusive industries: Hollywood, the media, politics. In Australia, the shape of the Indian diaspora is somewhat different, because of the various waves of migration from the subcontinent, driven by the policies of the time.

The many faces of the diaspora

To understand Australia's Indian diaspora, it is vital to apprehend two things: its utter lack of homogeneity, and how migration patterns led to what is essentially a fragmented community.

Surjeet Dhanji from the University of Melbourne's Asialink centre has researched Indians in Australia, in particular the different migration waves and how they interact. She describes the 1970s – which began with around 10,000 Indian-born people in Australia and recorded marginal growth over the ensuing years – as the era of doctors. Australia badly needed skilled migrants, and so the first wave of post–White Australia migrants were often highly educated and qualified, and found jobs almost immediately. The next wave consisted of IT workers, entrepreneurs and technocrats, who arrived during the 1980s. Then the 1990s saw a wave of younger skilled migrants. "In this time of globalisation, every country was inviting skilled migrants to keep their economy floating," says Dhanji. "[Indian migrants] contributed to jobs – the IT sector thrived because of them. They're also known to start SMEs [small- and medium-sized enterprises], many of which are in the hospitality sector. They own businesses and employ people."

By 2000, the Indian-born population was around 37,000. At the latest count, in June 2020, that number was 721,000. That's an almost twentyfold increase. And that is not taking into account second-generation Indian Australians, and Indian-heritage arrivals from elsewhere, such as Fiji, Malaysia, Singapore and the United Kingdom. It is also not factoring in other migrants from South Asia, such as Nepalis – a fast-growing community – Pakistanis, Bangladeshis and Sri Lankans. As the artist Sapna Chandu puts it, "Now when you walk down the street, it's a sea of brown."

The reason for this is economic: for Australia, more migrants means more workers, new businesses, more jobs. And India – where

English is widely spoken, where there is some semblance of cultural affinity (well, there's cricket, at least) and a young, dynamic and aspirational population – is perfectly positioned to be a source of future Australians.

Australia's economic future is linked to non-white migration; that point is inescapable. Several successive federal budgets have made this connection, trumpeting steadily high intakes of skilled migrants – currently around 160,000 per year – and, despite what rogue politicians or talkback hosts might say, there is no doubt that mass Indian migration is here to stay. India is the largest source of permanent migrants to Australia and accounts for the largest number of new Australian citizens.

"When we grew up it was like, 'Spot the Indian,' and then we'd all stare at each other because, you know, it was like, 'Look, there's another Indian!' So for our generation, it's quite profound," says Chandu.

My parents tell me that when they first arrived in Australia, half a century ago now, if they saw another brown person on the street they'd rush to greet them, and perhaps invite them over for dinner. Now the pendulum has swung sharply in the other direction, to the point where Indians complain that they come to Australia in the hopes of meeting and mixing with people of different backgrounds, only to find themselves in workplaces and social circles that are almost entirely Indian. Their social groups might feature a Bangladeshi or a Pakistani for some diversity – certainly more than they'd get at home – but all would be students, in their twenties and thirties, working crazy hours, and all bound by one thing: the quest for permanent residency.

This is just one aspect of the fragmentation. The Indians who have received that marvellous stroke of luck to have made it, with a job and permanent-resident status, even citizenship, quickly hive off into social groups that align with where they come from: north or south India, the state, the sub-region, the religion. Jayant Bapat is deeply involved with Maharashtra Mandal, a community group exclusively for arrivals from Maharashtra state: they gather, speak Marathi, eat Maharashtrian dishes such as *puran poli* (a sweet chapati) and *misal pav* (a spicy potato curry) that will never feature on the menu of your local Indian restaurant, discuss regional politics and tell jokes only they understand. The Indian Australian community is now so fragmented, Bapat tells me, that there is a club exclusively for people from the city of Nagpur. "It's good for them, but it means they hardly meet [other] Australian people." (Eventually they do, or their children do, he concedes, as 80 per cent of the weddings he conducts are mixed.) He worries that Indians' habit of siloing into niche communities is ultimately detrimental. "We live in these bubbles. And I don't know that's the right thing for a multicultural society." It also means that non–Indian Australians are shut out of events such as Diwali or Holi or other forms of cultural sharing.

The different Indian Australian communities don't really talk to each other. The different waves don't really talk to each other. The children born to first-generation migrants who came to Australia half a century ago might consider themselves to have a foot in each camp, yet may struggle to relate to a newly arrived migrant from their own generation.

There's a paragraph in the Aravind Adiga novel *Amnesty* (2020) that captures this situation perfectly: the protagonist, a visa-less Sri Lankan man in Sydney, categorises the other brown men "in a white man's city", describing "the ostentatiously indifferent *I've got nothing in common with you, mate* glances of the Australian-born children of doctors in Mosman or Castle Hill", dubbing them Icebox Indians. I cringed when I read this – because I know it to be true.

As such, it means that for this article I am forced to trawl Facebook groups to find newly arrived Indians to interview. One person who responds to my callout is Gourav Panchal, and we end up speaking on the phone for hours – both of us, I suspect, in thrall to this opportunity to communicate across the divide.

Panchal, twenty-four, desperately wants to settle in Australia. Hailing from Karnal in Haryana state, on the outskirts of Delhi – one of India's most socially regressive regions – he loves Australia's geography, wide open spaces and general open-mindedness. He came here as a student, his fees funded by his parents' life savings, to study a master's degree in environmental engineering at the University of Western Australia. He completed his degree a few months ago, and now he's on a bridging visa and working two jobs, up to fifteen hours a day, six days a week: during the day at an electronics factory in western Sydney owned by Indian brothers, and in the evenings at Woolworths.

His decision to leave his home country and settle abroad was motivated by a few factors beyond the economic. "I have always had a great love of the English language and Western culture – as a kid I'd watch television and think *I want to be part of that world*," he says during our late-night phone chat, the only time he has free in his punishing schedule. He also wanted to get away from what he saw as the petty concerns of his neighbourhood: "Like, if you park your car in front of their house they'll fight, they'll want to kill others over it."

The overwhelming reason, though, was to escape India's fierce competition for jobs and financial stability. India has a youth bulge, with around 600 million people under twenty-five – and increasingly, they're turning their backs on farming and are getting educated, in the hopes of moving a rung or three up the ladder. The problem is, with around 25 million people entering the job market each year, there simply aren't the jobs to go around.

What does this mean for someone like Panchal?

"See, ma'am, it's like this. I graduate from Haryana, I apply for jobs. There is *huge* competition for even ordinary jobs. So I go to Mumbai and I get a job – let's say it's 25,000 rupees [around AU$450] a month salary. Mumbai is an expensive place – even renting a room and buying basic groceries isn't covered by that amount. So you're still asking your family for support to live there. And then if you make even a small mistake, you're out, because you're so replaceable.

"So how are you going to create a life out of that? People realise that it's not worth it to compete for something that's not even going to give you the basic needs of life."

Panchal is trying to build up a financial buffer that will see him through whatever comes next, whether it is more study or an unpaid internship. For him and his peers, it's vital to do an internship to get a job, as employers, he says, only really value domestic experience. The internships are gruelling: full-time unpaid work, which would-be migrants must supplement with at least ten hours of paid work each week to cover their basic living expenses. Panchal knows someone who gave up a well-paid job as a petrol-station manager to do an unpaid internship; it's a struggle, he says.

Panchal speaks English beautifully, his clipped accent belying an upper-middle social class and a good education, which is noteworthy for his part of India, where Hindi is far more widely spoken than English. He speaks formally, peppering his conversation with "ma'am". He is thoughtful and intelligent, and as we speak I think how it must be galling for someone as educated as he to have to work unskilled jobs – although, he assures me, he doesn't mind, and he is treated and paid well.

"We don't have any political voice at all ... we're not one country, one people"

I then think about how much energy Australia puts into forging bilateral relations with India – with around fifty diplomats in four missions in India, it is a top diplomatic priority for Australia. Yet Australia has this incredible resource: Indian people, fantastically networked across regions, industries, religions, languages, communities – right here under its nose, in plain sight in supermarkets, or driving Ubers, or in petrol stations. And begging for opportunities.

And therein lies the rub. Talking to Indians in Australia, one thing becomes clear: this hunger to migrate has been thoroughly exploited by Australia. We have set the intake pipeline so that it benefits Australia at every stage. First, students pay huge sums of money to study here (usually it's their parents' life savings, or land is sold to finance the fees). Then, while they're studying, they provide a cheap, readily available and compliant source of unskilled labour. After graduation, they take on unpaid internships of three to six months, living off their savings, or fitting in overnight shifts at the servo to pay the rent. Then they emerge, fully trained with an Australian education, ready to join the workforce, fuelling our economic growth. At every stage, the benefits are stacked in Australia's favour. The house always wins.

I present this idea to Panchal, who goes quiet, and then speaks with a new urgency and emotion. "See, the government here gets big revenue from students, billions of dollars each year. But they've made the policies so strict around residency and citizenship. They want to bring people here, as students or skilled people, they want people to work here, then pay taxes and spend their life savings here, but when it comes to offering residency or citizenship, the government is not very flexible on that." Panchal knows people who are highly skilled, have met all the requirements and have been in Australia for more than a decade, and still don't have residency. "Till they have it, they can't plan their future. They can't grab opportunities. They can't buy a house. They can't plan their career or future at all.

"I know people here, they meet all the criteria, but as soon as they meet it, the criteria changes, the bar moves a bit higher. You used to need 60 or 65 points, and that in itself is high, it's hard to get. But now it's raised to 95, 100 points. To get that, you have to do jobs here, and do unpaid internships. You understand? It's a whole chain."

(I checked the Home Affairs website for details on the points needed: for the skilled independent visa, subclass 189, it says: "Points criteria are assessed at the time of invitation.")

Panchal is frustrated with the way the system has inbuilt barriers for someone like him. Still, he is determined to stay the course. He speaks about the moments that remind him of why he came, like his first visit to Palm Beach, north of Sydney. "I climbed up and looked down at the beach, and I felt like: *my whole life I wanted to come to a place like this.*"

Unheard and unrepresented

The growth of the Indian community in Australia has had one particularly undesirable impact: a rise in domestic violence within its confines. There is little firm data on the topic, but it is known that Indian women, as a group, are the second-highest callers to the 1800RESPECT line after Australian-born women. Earlier this year it was revealed that Indian victims of family violence formed the highest group receiving visas allowing them to stay in Australia, with 280 Indians successful in their applications since 2012–13. There were also the revelations of a suicide cluster of Indian women in one part of Melbourne in 2018 and 2019. It is clear that Indian women who come to Australia as brides are deeply vulnerable.

The violence is often directly linked to dowry abuse. This form of abuse occurs when, after an initial payment – by the bride's family to the groom, or to his family – the demands for money continue to a point where the wife feels threatened and unsafe.

Melbourne psychologist Manjula O'Connor has long worked with women in crisis, supporting their mental health and rehabilitation as well as running awareness and prevention workshops. "If [the wife] does not comply with the demands, that leads to domestic violence or abuse or servitude, and other controlling behaviours – controlling her bank account, controlling her access to parents and social support networks," says O'Connor. "The mental health effects are very significant, including PTSD, even suicide."

She is calling for tighter legislation. Victoria has legislated against this form of coercive control, and the New South Wales government is debating whether to criminalise such behaviour; if successful, it would help foster public recognition of the issue of dowry abuse. "Laws dictate our behaviour, and the laws would send a clear signal to our perpetrators here in Australia that this kind of behaviour is unacceptable … we need judges who understand and juries who understand what dowry abuse is and how it can put the life of a woman at risk."

It is important to differentiate between dowries and dowry abuse: a dowry is a gift from parents to a bride to help set her up in her new life, although in practice it is usually taken by the groom's family. It might come in the form of cash, gold jewellery, a car or a fridge, even clothing. It is a practical reflection of the fact that a bride is joining her husband's household, and while the amount is pegged to her husband's perceived value, the dowry is ultimately hers. Dowry abuse is when demands for payment continue after the marriage and escalate dangerously.

I ask O'Connor about a case in which a court found a man not guilty of murder after his wife was seen running out of her house engulfed in flames and died shortly afterwards. She had previously made allegations of domestic violence. O'Connor's voice cracks with emotion. "I've seen hundreds of women of South Asian origin, and they feel utterly, utterly helpless, and unsupported by the system."

Indians will constitute a greater part of Australia's population than ever before

Victoria's *Family Violence Protection Act 2008* now includes "dowry coercion" as an example of economic abuse. O'Connor welcomes this, but wants to see it enshrined in federal family law. She points out that even when a bride manages to leave an abusive household, her dowry, her entire fortune, is left behind. Police in Victoria are thoroughly educated about dowry abuse, she says, and she is pleased to see that New South Wales is currently educating its force. This is important because in cases where a husband might claim that a wife has attempted suicide, the attending officers need to understand that there may be reasons not to take this explanation at face value.

A game-changer, of course, would be political representation for Indians – whether Indian-born or second- or third-generation. The paucity of Indian political activity in Australia is extremely evident, particularly when compared to the Chinese community, which has federal representation and representation at lower levels of government too. There is Dave Sharma, of course, born Devanand to an ethnic Indian father from Trinidad and an Australian mother, who is often described as "an Indian-Australian politician"; but there is no evidence that he has waved the flag (or plans to) in parliament on behalf of the Indian diaspora. Former Tasmanian senator Lisa Singh, the first Australian of South Asian descent to be elected to federal parliament, spoke about these issues when she was in office, but she lost her seat in the 2019 federal election after being placed fourth on Labor's Tasmanian Senate ticket.

Both Jayant Bapat and Surjeet Dhanji want more political representation for Indian Australians. Bapat links the issues of regional and linguistic silos to the lack of a political voice, saying that Australian politicians don't come to events in the Indian Australian community anymore. This wasn't always the case; growing up, I would regularly see politicians, including then immigration and multicultural affairs minister Philip Ruddock, at community events. (I have a strong memory of him and his wife, both sporting floral garlands, grimacing stoically one Diwali as the event devolved into an extremely raucous Bollywood club night.) "We don't have any political voice at all," Bapat says. "And that's because we're not one country, one people."

Earlier this year, Dhanji wrote a strongly worded piece for *The Indian Express*, an Indian daily newspaper, asking, "Where are the Indian-Australian politicians?" In it, she quotes from interviews with unsuccessful Indian Australian political candidates, many of whom said preselection remains a significant hurdle, as does the lack of social and professional networks that connect them to political parties. She writes:

> Australia has neglected to embrace cultural and ethnic diversity in parliament to the same degree as nations such as Britain and the US, where politicians from Indian migrant backgrounds were elected to government as early as the 1890s and 1957 respectively, when the Indian diaspora was comparatively minuscule.

She suggests that parties should work hard to attract, train and retain culturally diverse members to create a pipeline of candidates for future political positions.

The flight ban

It is a strange time to be writing a feature examining the Indian diaspora and speculating on its possible future. Earlier this year, as the Delta variant was ripping through parts of India, the Australian government, fearful of the virus jumping ship into our ports, halted flights from India. Many Indians were trapped either in their country of origin or helplessly watching from Australia, hoping that elderly parents or siblings wouldn't succumb to the virus.

The spread of Covid-19 in India might have ebbed, but the pain has not. As I write this, a recent post on a Facebook forum for Indians in Australia reads: "I recently lost my father and couldn't travel to India to be with him in his last moments. The grief and guilt is eating me up from inside, that I couldn't say goodbye to him. My question is not about getting an exemption to travel, but how to get over this guilt? How to cope with this agony of being so far from home?" A handful of comments describe similar experiences. "Lost mum to Covid. Couldn't kiss her goodbye. Feel cheated," says one. It is difficult to read, and worse yet to contemplate the depth of their suffering.

Undoubtedly, the way Australia treated international students during the initial lockdown, followed by the travel ban – short as it was – affected how Indians view the country, either as a place to trade or to settle. But will that have any impact on migration levels? It is too early to tell, and won't be known at least until late 2022, when the latest census results will be released. Bapat believes, based on his conversations with people in his community, that Indians are disgruntled but will continue to seek to come here. Despite every-thing, Australia holds better prospects for their future than India ever will.

If there is an upside to the crisis, it is this: the Sikh Volunteers. The group, which distributes meals and groceries to people in need, has emerged as one of the shining lights, first of the bushfire crisis and then of the pandemic. Sikh Volunteers has done much for intercommunity relations, and I'm looking forward to a future when they might, say, get a mid-game standing ovation the next time Australia meets India at the MCG.

The flight ban raised strong opinions for and against, but it also highlighted just how far Australia has come in terms of accepting its Indian population. The vast majority of the discourse was in support of the Indians. It is clear that Australians, of Indian and non-Indian heritage alike, have accepted that Indians are vital to the country's economic future as well as to its social fabric, now and beyond.

Australia's future Indian-ness

A study published in *Genus* last year projected that Australia's Indian-born population will rise to 2.3 million by 2066, based on migration patterns and mortality rates. The authors admit this is far from assured, as migration policy and triggers may change over time. Still, even on a conservative reckoning, Indians will constitute a greater part of Australia's population than ever before.

This is already having an impact on some parts of life – such as the construction of new housing developments across Melbourne's outer suburbs, or funeral homes offering vegetarian options for Hindu services.

If we look ahead, say twenty years into the future, it is evident how Australia will evolve, at least on the surface: more hybrid restaurants; more sporting cooperation; a few Indian words might even sneak into the vernacular. But will Australians be open to taking on some of the less accessible elements of Indian-ness, such as their deep religiosity or their classism? Who will have to adapt most: Indian migrants or the wider Australian society?

Kwality Chai creator Sapna Chandu believes that elements of Indian culture will continue to be folded into Australian culture, almost by stealth, to a point where they merge and meld to create something new. "Look what's happened with yoga. Then there's the Color Run, which was inspired by Holi. It starts with these activities and then there's a bit more depth into the culture. Sometimes it's just that certain activities are appropriated and then take place in this new integrated sort of culture."

With luck, this new integrated culture might also mean she can one day order a decent masala chai. ■

TIKTOK WARS

Why India's youth are hating on China

Snigdha Poonam

> *Let our Asian millions sing*
> *Tribute to the mighty pact*
> *Which shall ever be intact*
> *Pandit Nehru, Chou En-lai*
> *Hindi-Chini bhai-bhai*
> **—Hindi-Chini poem by Harindranath**
> **Chattopadhyay, 1954**

> *The whole world is against you*
> *You have only Pakistan*
> *You attack from behind*
> *Because you will be thrashed upfront*
> *Everyone has seen your true colours*
> **—Anti-China poem on Twitter and Instagram,**
> **Lokesh Indoura, 2020**

On 19 June 2020, an Indian man dressed as Xi Jinping walked a busy Kolkata street ahead of a mob carrying a wooden gallows. He wore a black suit, a red tie and a solemn expression. The stage makeup and bouffant hair made him look more like a vintage Hollywood star than the Chinese president, but that did not deter his angry audience. For his finale, at a fixed point the performer stepped into the gallows, slid the thick rope around his neck and tilted it to the left, sticking out his tongue to complete the effect.

Just four days before, Chinese and Indian forces had fought by the Galwan River, which divides the two nations through mountainous territory. The clashes killed twenty Indian soldiers (China reported no casualties at that time). Their bodies arrived in Delhi wrapped in the Indian flag and their cremations were covered on national television. Not since 1962, during a border war between the Asian neighbours, had Indians demonstrated such outrage towards China. Protests broke out across the country. Thousands of people wanted to see the Chinese premier dead. Many of them played out their hateful fantasy by erecting his effigy, pelting it with stones, carrying it on funeral biers and, in multiple locations, burning it in city centres.

"Indians, we are a sensitive people," R.J. Raunac, a Delhi breakfast-radio host and one of India's youth icons, told me. "We love our country. When something like this happens, when we see a martyr's last rites, people get emotional and that's how they form their opinion, whether about China or Pakistan or any other country. After some days, if it's a bubble, it will burst."

But this one hasn't burst yet.

*

More than a year after the Galwan clashes, the anti-China sentiment continues to grow. In 2019, only 23 per cent of Indians surveyed by the Pew Research Center saw China favourably. In 2021, according to the latest Munich Security Report, 78 per cent of Indian respondents named "Chinese aggression" as the main risk they faced, followed by the coronavirus pandemic.

The Indian state isn't fuelling this perception. The last time Prime Minister Narendra Modi spoke to Indians about the conflict was on 19 June 2020, while fake Xi Jinpings were handing themselves over to the crowds. In a televised statement, Modi acknowledged that "the entire country is hurt and angry at the steps taken by China". He hasn't said a word about it since, not even on the first anniversary. "There was no comment from the government. Not one tweet," said Suhasini Haidar, diplomatic affairs editor at *The Hindu*, on the panel discussion "One Year After Galwan", hosted by Delhi's Centre for Policy Research. She compared that to Modi's messaging after the 2019 terrorist attack in Pulwama, a district of Jammu and Kashmir, in which eleven Indian soldiers died; he paid tribute to the martyrs on the first and second anniversaries of the suicide bombing. "I don't think it's just by chance. The message is that India wants to play it down. That's what it wants to convey domestically."

It's tried-and-tested caution, said Tanvi Madan, senior fellow at the Brookings Institution. "One of the things India and China's governments have learnt from history is that once you take it public, the conflict gets harder to resolve." She suggested that the anti-China anger in India started before the Galwan clashes. "The big shift happened in early 2020 because of Covid. This was people just being really upset, particularly at the lack of transparency. This was before Donald Trump was calling it the China virus, etc. You saw a lot more of that coming from India than you did in the United States at that time. It did not seem to be very organised. What really struck me was this wasn't just coming from the [political] right. Even [politically] moderate people expressed sentiments that were surprising in their intensity, and once the boundary crisis happened, you saw it go even further."

Once sparked, the sentiment was fuelled by a range of people who feed off public opinion: film stars, news anchors, meme makers. Street protests swiftly gave way to internet outrage. The charge was led by online influencers selling a new idea of patriotism to India's overwhelmingly young internet users (more than 50 per cent of its 504 million online population is between twenty and thirty-nine years of age). So far, many of them have only seen China as a place that makes things that bring joy to their lives. For as long as they can remember, they have used Chinese smartphones, plugged in Chinese speakers and played Chinese video games, which they streamed on Chinese apps. The border clashes changed that. It made them question their reliance on a nation whose alleged interests, whether territorial or economic, go against India's. To find the answers, they are looking to the same online idols that tell them which shoes to buy and which songs to listen to.

Wakening India's youth

R.J. Raunac became a public figure playing pranks on radio. For more than ten years, he has played practical jokes on members of the public for India's most popular radio channel, Red FM 93.5, while affecting a baby voice. His moniker, Bauaa ("kid"), evokes light entertainment and laughter. The 36-year-old uses the same persona on his YouTube channel, which has 2.9 million subscribers. Some of his most-watched videos comment on Bollywood and cricket. But after last June, he started making videos about China. "As an Indian, and as an aware Indian, you want to engage with whatever is happening in the country. The border conflict between China and India was one thing that was in people's minds," he said. Indeed, in the months following the Galwan River clashes, "China roasting" became a trend on Indian YouTube.

Indian protesters began to burn anything Chinese-made they could lay their hands on

"China has come up only recently on the hate radar," said Vishal Sharma, who leads Hindustani Biradari, a nation-building initiative headquartered in Agra, in the northern state of Uttar Pradesh. "It started when the Chinese army extended its reach into the Tawang Lake area. The hate for China has only developed in the past three to four years. Before that, China was a very good partner for India. This is a very new thing for India."

But anti-China sentiment has come and gone in waves ever since October 1962, when the People's Liberation Army invaded the Indian territories of Ladakh and Arunachal Pradesh. Over the following weeks, India lost 43,000 square kilometres of land and 250 soldiers before China declared a ceasefire. "Although brief, the war left a psychological scar on the Indian government and people," Tansen Sen writes in his 2017 book *India, China, and the World*. The armed conflict laid to waste the Panchsheel Agreement that India and China had signed in 1954 outlining the Five Principles of Peaceful Co-Existence, sparking years of state-sponsored exchange trips and sugary poems. "The legacy defining the contemporary ROI-PRC relationship is not the two thousand/three thousand years of friendly exchanges," Sen writes, but "the discontent emerging out of the 1962 war and the persistent territorial dispute."

Even though boundary issues became a feature of the India–China relationship, shots were never fired, and outrage was limited to security experts – until now. "Indian soldiers being killed does change the sentiment," Tanvi Madan said.

On 6 June, a week before the anniversary of the Galwan conflict, R.J. Raunac posted a video titled "Does China want India's destruction?" Beforehand, he had asked his followers on social media what they wished to know about India–China relations. "People had many questions. But most of them asked: what is China's issue with the entire world? Because you see so many clashes. With Russia over territory, with the US over the economy. People wanted to know about the China–Pakistan Economic Corridor. Is it a trap for Pak? Can India be an alternate power? Can it tackle China?" The video features his conversation with a former officer of the Indian army, Gaurav Arya, internet-famous himself for conjuring a parallel universe in which India wins every battle. Talking to Raunac, Arya advocates India leave behind "decency" in dealing with China. "*Jo dharm ki ladai hai who rakshason se nahin ladi jati.* (You can't fight a battle of principles with demons.)"

Raunac argues the aim of his videos is not to depict China in a bad light but to wake up young Indians. "We should make ourselves more powerful to tackle them. You don't have to burn effigies all the time. Can you inspire our youth to create an alternative?" he said.

Close to 400,000 followers have watched his last video; he believes at least some of them are with him. "The youth are asking, 'How can India become a superpower? How can it become self-reliant?' Unfortunately, it's only when an incident happens that the youth are motivated, and they speak loudly about it. It's disappointing, but we trust our youth, and we have seen quite a lot of change."

A message to China

Quiet descended on the border, yet the burning continued for weeks. After the effigies turned to ashes, Indian protesters began to burn anything Chinese-made they could lay their hands on: mobile phones, remote controls, teddy bears.

As enemy nations go, Indians today regard Pakistan and China as equally dangerous, said Surya Narayan, a Bengaluru-based convenor of the Bajrang Dal, a militant wing of the Hindu-nationalist Rashtriya Swayamsevak Sangh, whose cadres went on a burning spree across

India. Others say that after the clashes, anti-China sentiment overtook anti-Pakistan sentiment.

Tanvi Madan does not believe these two rivalries overlap in the Indian imagination. "For all the adversarial discussion on the India–Pakistan front, the societies are far more familiar with each other. Whether it's over cricket or food or blaming the British together, you think of the other side as familiar. There is some shared history. You may see them as enemies, but you see them as people." That familiarity is missing from the India–China relationship, she pointed out. "It's very easy to basically conflate the Chinese state and Chinese people. In some ways, that makes the anti-China sentiment and Othering become even more acute when it does rise."

When burning wasn't an option, people simply threw Chinese goods out of their windows, from television sets to water coolers. Many vowed not to buy any more Chinese-made products. In September 2020, Vishal Sharma, vice-chairman of the cultural organisation Hindustani Biradari, called a web conference to issue a boycott of Chinese products across the expansive Braj region in Uttar Pradesh. Visibly furious, Sharma dismissed the idea of "Hindi–Chini friendship" (referencing the popular slogan Prime Minister Jawaharlal Nehru coined on a visit to China in 1954) as a myth created by Nehru and Zhou Enlai. He accused China of spying on Indian households through its electronic products. "The sentiment had formed in response to the Chinese aggression at the border. The technological dominance China has over us, we felt we had to balance that. That's why we called for a ban," he said, looking back on that day.

Feeling the pressure, the Indian government placed restrictions on trade – barring public-sector companies from signing new contracts with Chinese entities, curtailing the flow of Chinese capital into private enterprises and ordering e-commerce sites to specify their products' country of origin. This wasn't the first time border tensions had provoked Indians to call for an economic boycott of China; but as proved again and again, it's easier said than done. Between 2018 and 2020, bilateral trade between China and India decreased by 18 per cent, but as Indians scanned their houses for Chinese products to disown, China was still India's second-largest commercial partner. No matter how many speeches Narendra Modi makes about self-reliance, India's growth can't go on without the imports of auto parts and pharma ingredients from across the contentious border.

"From 2003 to 2007, there was a gap between the capabilities of India and China, whether on the economy or the military, but we were seen as shrinking that gap. The Chinese economy was slowing down. The Indian economy was growing at the rate of 8 to 9 per cent per annum. In the international discourse, India was the next China," said Shyam Saran, a former foreign secretary of India, at the Centre for Policy Research's forum. That changed after 2008: "What has happened since is that the gap between India and China has expanded. And it's expanding even further."

Across all dimensions of power, said Taylor Fravel, an expert on China's foreign policy, "China views itself in a position of strength, India having far less leverage or options with which to change the situation".

But in India, the mood was grim and the public had to be placated.

On 29 June 2020, the Indian government banned fifty-three Chinese apps from all mobile stores in India. Many of the apps boasted millions of users; some of them counted India as their biggest market.

The fact that millions of young Indians spent most of their time on these Chinese apps – singing, dancing, livestreaming, gaming – had come up in the parliament even before the Galwan episode. India's self-styled nationalists could make their peace with the import of goods because it happened outside the public view, but few of them could claim not to have seen a teenager creating a TikTok video.

"I am filled with shame looking at the young generation of India. What are they doing? How well are they delivering their duty towards their nation?" said Balram Dhangar, a former commando of one of India's paramilitary forces, on Facebook Live a day before the clashes. He runs a physical training academy in Rajasthan for young men who want to enter the armed forces, but he wields more influence posting motivational videos for his army of Facebook followers. His young, predominantly male fans admire the hyper-masculine persona he showcases online: twirling his handlebar moustache, performing hand-stands from a jump start, roving farmlands with a gun strapped to his chest. Last year, Dhangar launched a youth force, Mission Hindustan, dedicated to nation-building. "It's my ultimate goal to make the youth aware of India's interests," he said in a phone interview. Dhangar believes nothing hampers India's interests more than its youth "singing and dancing on Chinese apps".

Yet they were doing it all around him. By 2020, Chinese apps had reached the smallest of Indian villages. Tens of thousands of youngsters were earning their income as creators, livestreamers and influencers on these apps that asked for no other credential than a phone number. "TikTok made so many people famous who lacked any other option to show their talent. It made stars out of villagers," said Sameera Khan, a former TikTok creator.

Dhangar disagrees with that view. "The Indian soldier stands at the border and lays down his life. The Indian youth enables the apps from the same country to make profits. That is what makes China economically strong," he said in his livestream. "And that's how they are able to dare us at the border. The reason is our youth. If this money stayed in India, it would make our economy stronger. But do the youth care? No, they want to sing and dance. No time to pay respects to martyrs."

Banning popular Chinese apps was the easiest way for India to show that it was prepared to teach China a lesson. The Ministry of Electronics and Information Technology issued a single order to Google and Apple, and millions woke the next day unable to access their morning entertainment. Dhangar was thrilled. "Today, my chest expanded to 56 inches," he said in a video posted the day after, referring to Modi's boasts about his chest size, which have taken hold among his supporters as a symbol of his strongman image. The former soldier, whose videos often advise followers on exercises to expand their chests, felt a burden off his own. "I used to worry when I saw what the

Indian youth was up to. It used to pain me. But the prime minister has delivered a fitting slap to the enemy. He has broken their back with this ban. My dream of many years has come true. Now let us see China try to threaten us."

Over the next five months, the government banned hundreds more Chinese apps "for engaging in activities prejudicial to India's sovereignty, integrity, defence, security and public order". Domestic technology firms were told to create made-in-India alternatives as part of an "*atmanirbhar* [self-reliance] application challenge". Dozens sprang up in response, offering attractions copied line of code by line of code from the banned Chinese apps. On 30 August 2020, in his monthly radio address, Modi congratulated Indians on their newfound freedom from Chinese apps: "Dear countrymen, everyone acknowledges the capability of Indians to offer innovation and solutions. When there is dedication and sensitivity, the power becomes limitless."

The message was directed at India's youth, many of whom were still struggling to come to terms with the ban. "Until this moment, there had been no discussion about how these apps were collecting our data. Suddenly we were told that this data was going to China," said Khan, who had five million followers on one app when it was banned. "It was dearer to us than our lives. But we made the sacrifice for the nation," the 27-year-old Mumbai resident, who became TikTok famous while acting out Bollywood-style emotional scenarios, said. It wasn't a small sacrifice. "For millions of people, it was their only world. The community of creators worked like a family."

That family was now deeply divided: nation or dreams? This divide was evident on social media, where two categories of videos were going viral: one advised internet users on how to identify and block Chinese apps on mobile stores, and the other offered tricks for how to find and operate banned ones.

Khan says none of the Indian copies of TikTok can beat the original. She was invited to join a made-in-India short video app called Mauj, but she hasn't been able to attract more than 200,000 followers yet. "We will always be TikTokers. That tag will never go away. The new apps in the market are only promoting those who were made famous by TikTok. For the new users, it's not easy to rise from scratch," she said.

More than a year after she was locked out of her account, she wonders if the ban did India any good. "So many dreams were shattered so that India could register a win against China. Our loyalty is first with the nation, but what we still don't know is how the nation benefited from our sacrifice. It's not clear to us."

Waiting for change

Khan is not alone in her confusion. A year after thousands of Indians took up the cudgels against China, many wonder if India can defy its powerful neighbour. Vishal Sharma is one of them. Today, he is not sure his call for a ban on Chinese products was practical. "The anti-China sentiment has been negated. It's almost over."

Sharma still goes out of his way to pick Indian products over Chinese ones, even avoiding products assembled from Chinese parts.

"If I have to buy something made outside of India, I will buy it from Taiwan or Singapore. Not from China. Call it pride in my own country," he said. But he has given up on converting others. "Our call for the ban carried through 30 to 40 per cent, but not to the extent that anybody would have liked it to. In today's global economy, we cannot force anybody to use one particular brand or product. Or buy from one geographical region. Bans don't work. It should be voluntary. If you take one simple example, the sale of Chinese-made mobile phones is higher today than it has been in the last two to three years."

Balram Dhangar too has stopped his spiels against the dangers of singing and dancing for likes and views. "If China apps are banned, Indian apps will come. If Indian apps are banned, some other apps will come. No one can stop this chain. The youth today will search for entertainment options no matter what. What can anyone do? We can't tie them up."

In June, China overtook the United States to become India's leading trade partner as imports, including those of essential medical supplies, rose through the first year of the pandemic. In the fiscal year 2020–21, bilateral trade stood at US$86.4 billion, defying India's repeated efforts to economically "decouple" from China. To be sure, India and China are far from being friends. Their premiers have met a few times for multilateral discussions, including BRICS (a grouping of five major emerging economies, which also includes Brazil, Russia and South Africa). But diplomatic ties remain frigid. In May 2021, India's foreign minister,

Subrahmanyam Jaishankar, admitted the relationship is going through a "very difficult phase" even as their armies continue to disengage at the border.

While neither nation wants to stoke the fire, a section of the Indian population waits for revenge. Their hope centres on Modi, whose domestic image is built on claims of "surgical strikes" against India's enemies. "Earlier we had no hopes of it, but after Modi's arrival, there is a strong feeling of nationalism, of national security. People have been able to call out China," said Prakash Shrivastava, a social media volunteer for Rashtriya Swayamsevak Singh. He claims now is the perfect time for India to take down China. The ammunition: Covid-19. "The anti-China sentiment has been building up. Covid is the last nail in the coffin."

On 25 May 2021, Shrivastava, who recently left his corporate job to focus on social work, lost his brother to Covid-19. By official estimates, as of mid-September 2021, 441,000 Indians had died in the pandemic. Even before his personal tragedy, Shrivastava was tweeting every anti-China theory on the spread of the virus, from lab leak to bioweapon. Indians add a sizeable volume of the tweets that make Covid-19 hashtags such as #Chinamustpay trend on Twitter. "I believed Donald Trump from the beginning," Shrivastava said. He says he speaks for his social network – online and offline. "The bioweapon theory is taking hold in India very strongly." What they were waiting for is "someone to stand up to China". By the looks of it, Modi might keep them waiting for the foreseeable future.

Sameera Khan is also waiting, and she is not alone, either. If India and China remain on friendly business terms, she and her family of creators hopes the apps will be back. "No one I know has deleted TikTok. They keep the app on their phones even if they can't log in. They could delete it, but they fear if they do, it will be lost forever." ∎

THE VIEW FROM INDIA

Kinship in the pushback
against Beijing

Harsh V. Pant

In today's ever-so-volatile Indo-Pacific, India's relationship with Australia is far closer than it has been at any time in history. The two nations share a similar assessment of the region, their strategic partners are the same, they have common political values and their economic partnership is growing. Yet this level of comfort is extraordinary given how distant the two nations seemed just a decade ago.

Earlier this century, as the Indian middle class expanded, an increasing number of students began to pursue education abroad. Australia became a preferred destination. In 2009, some 92,106 Indian students were enrolled in Australia – a huge increase from 23,491 students just three years previously. But this growing interaction between Australians and Indians rapidly turned sour due to a series of attacks on Indian students. In 2009–10 alone, more than 1450 cases of violence against Indians in Australia were recorded. The Australian government tried to downplay it by framing these attacks as crimes triggered by economic anxieties, arguing that the targeting of Indians was coincidental and circumstantial. Only a few instances of this unprovoked violence, they claimed, were racially motivated.

But many Indians in Australia, as well as some media outlets and Opposition leaders, refused to buy it. And this narrative of Australia's cruelty soon gained traction in India. The Indian media started to cover the issue almost daily, keeping a tally of these violent incidents. Major newspapers ran stories of attacks on their front pages. A television anchor on the popular Times Now channel called the Australian authorities liars, accusing them of preying on Indians selfishly, for economic gain. The term "curry bashings" – seldom used outside India to refer to attacks on Indians – was seized upon by the Indian media and became common. One cartoon depicted the Australian police as the Ku Klux Klan, attracting diplomatic protests from Australia.

This coverage caused panic and alarm for prospective students and underscored growing negative perceptions of Australia. In May 2009, Bollywood actor Amitabh Bachchan rejected an honorary doctorate from an Australian university for his contribution to cinema, citing Australia's unjust treatment of Indian students. Bollywood movies such as *Crook* (2010) depicted the attacks in Australia as racially motivated. As the public backlash grew, Indian political parties protested and high-level diplomatic and political talks were held between Australia and India. In 2010, the number of Indian students in Australia declined to 80,300, and by 2013 it dropped to 30,400.

The saga reflected the social and political gulf that existed between India and Australia, in which each was stymied by a lack of understanding of the other. This disconnect was telling, and it was not only playing out over Australia's treatment of its Indian students. It highlighted a wider strategic divergence between New Delhi and Canberra.

Strategic dissonance

In November 2009, Australian prime minister Kevin Rudd and Indian prime minister Manmohan Singh decided to elevate their security ties to the level of a "strategic partnership". Despite the release of a joint statement foregrounding their "shared interests and shared values", nothing substantive came of this move. In truth, it was Canberra's attempt to reach out to New Delhi, but India did not see Australia as a priority and was reluctant to reciprocate.

This was part of a long pattern. Since 1986, no Indian prime minister had found time to visit Australia. As the Cold War thawed, India and Australia began to engage even as many in India continued to perceive Australia as a US stooge. But the relationship struggled to grow beyond "cricket, Commonwealth and curry". After India's 1998 nuclear tests, Canberra's reaction was extreme: then foreign minister Alexander Downer labelled the tests "outrageous", recalled the defence attaché from India and sent all Indian students at the Australian Defence College packing. It reflected a lack of sensitivity to India's genuine security concerns. Australia's vacillation over uranium sales to India in 2007 added to the mistrust – Australia came on board in 2011 after

India signed a nuclear deal with the United States, underscoring for many in New Delhi Australia's reluctance to show genuine independence in its foreign policy decisions.

But there was one idea that, for a fleeting moment, gave new purpose to the engagement between the two countries. The notion that four democracies – India, Japan, Australia and the United States – working together could maximise results for all gained traction during the humanitarian relief operations conducted after the 2004 Boxing Day tsunami. This "quad" grouping, promoted strongly by Japan's Shinzō Abe and gaining strength due to America's "pivot" to the Asia-Pacific, saw a variety of diplomatic and political interactions take place from mid-2006. In 2007, three of the states participated in the annual Malabar naval exercise for the first time. This had begun as a bilateral naval engagement between India and the United States in 1992, with Japan joining in 2015. But the first – albeit informal – meeting of the Quadrilateral Security Dialogue, in 2007 in Manila, attracted strong protests from China. Conscious of its relationship with China, Australia became the first country to withdraw from the Quad.

In India, this reinforced the perception that the Australian government was shifting to favour China. The view was reinforced by the Rudd government's decision not to sell uranium to India, which heightened concerns that Rudd's interests did not align with India's and widened the trust deficit between the two nations. Australia was widely seen in India as the key reason why the Quad did not take off, and Australia's continued engagement with the United States and Japan, combined with the lack of outreach to India, further shaped the perception that it had left India to fend off China alone. Strategic disconnect grew between the two nations as India rejected Rudd's proposed India–United States–Australia trilateral economic and security pact in 2011.

However, the limitations of the Quad 1.0 were evident from the very beginning. The member countries had no clear understanding of what the grouping meant for their strategic priorities and what purposes it would serve. Australia was not the only reason it did not fructify; China's high-decibel protests had all four nations worried, including India, which was loath to join any arrangement that would further complicate an already tenuous Sino–Indian relationship. The Indian government was reluctant to confront its domestic coalition partners, who were against moving closer to the West. In fact, Australia and India both lacked enthusiasm to commit to the Quad.

Australia's Defence minister, Brendon Nelson, stated in July 2007 that he had "reassured China that [the] so-called security quadrilateral dialogue with India is not something we are pursuing". Two months later, Shinzō Abe – credited with proposing the dialogue – resigned. In December 2007, the United States declared it was prioritising its trilateral engagement with Japan and Australia over the Quad. New Delhi's principle of strategic autonomy had already made it sceptical of the Quad, and the whole thing fell apart.

By the end of the 2000s, as the Quad faltered and the student attacks began, relations between India and Australia were at a low point. Yet in the past decade, both countries have undergone an unprecedented shift. Their strategic worldviews have changed and, as a result, so has the nature of their outreach to each other.

United by China

Due to China's aggressive posturing, India and Australia today share a concern about the stability of the region's maritime order. In 2014, during a historic address to a joint session of Australia's parliament, Indian prime minister Narendra Modi expressed his apprehension about the Indo-Pacific's security. "This vast region has many unsettled questions and new challenges. Historical differences persist despite growing interdependence … we worry about its access and security in our part of the world more than ever before," he said. Two years later, the 2016 Australian Defence White Paper recognised that "the region's seas and airspace are becoming more contested … as it does, several factors suggest we [would] face an increasingly complex and contested Indo–Pacific". The congruence of India and Australia's views about the geopolitical situation in the Indo-Pacific makes them natural partners.

It was this convergence that resulted in the reanimation of the Quad. In March 2018, China's foreign minister, Wang Yi, had referred to the Quad as nothing more than "sea foam on the Pacific and Indian oceans". But, unlike sea foam, it did not dissipate; instead, as China's foreign policy became more irresponsible and shortsighted, the once shaky foundations of the Quad strengthened. In March 2021, the Quad emerged as the first multilateral engagement of a new US administration.

When the Chinese foreign policy establishment looks back at recent history, it can be justifiably proud of its accomplishment in sowing the seeds of a new regional security architecture. The "Indo-Pacific" would have remained a concept in think-tank reports, and the Quad nothing more than a trial balloon, had it not been for China's aggression towards its neighbours over the last decade. Chinese belligerence in its land and maritime disputes, the increasingly questionable intent of its Belt and Road Initiative and its related debt-trap diplomacy all challenged the "peaceful rise of China" thesis. Consequently, Australia, India, Japan and the United States breathed new life into their security arrangements. Quad 2.0 started meeting biannually at a senior official level in 2017, and was upgraded to the ministerial level in 2019. At its core, it seeks to maintain and strengthen a rules-based regional maritime order to prevent instability by ensuring the principle of a Free and Open Indo-Pacific.

In 2020, the Quad held a virtual meeting – which also included Vietnam, New Zealand and South Korea – to strengthen inter-regional coordination in mitigating the impact of the Covid-19 pandemic. The agenda included vaccine development, repatriation of overseas citizens and minimising the economic fallout.

But it was the March 2021 virtual summit of the four leaders of the Quad countries that gave the security dialogue a renewed vigour. In their first joint statement, the leaders underlined their commitment "to advance security and prosperity and counter threats to both in the Indo-Pacific and beyond", as well as supporting "freedom of navigation and overflight, peaceful resolution of disputes, democratic values, and territorial integrity".

China, of course, took note and hit out at nations forming "enclosed small cliques", describing this as "the sure way to destroy the international order". It took aim at "certain countries" for being "keen to exaggerate and hype up the so-called 'China threat' to sow discord among regional countries, especially to disrupt their relations with China".

The agenda of the Quad 2.0, as outlined during the March summit, is expansive and stands on its own merits, without the crutch of the China threat. The leaders have been creative and realistic as they seek to offer an alternative form of regional governance to the smaller states in the Indo-Pacific. The main constraint on the Quad so far has not been China's rise but the unwillingness of other major regional players – including India and Australia – to do their bit in offering credible alternatives. It is not that China has been a playing a great strategic game; it is that others are conceding defeat before even making a move. That's being rectified now, and the consequences will be serious – for China, for smaller states and for the region at large.

The Quad members are trying to ensure that a rising China does not remain inimical to their interests. All states, major and minor, will continue to engage with China, but the battle is over who sets the terms of this engagement.

And it is here that India's role has been central. The 2020 border crisis (sparked by China's decision to alter the status quo along the contested Sino-Indian border) ushered in a shift in India's China policy. Yet even before that, New Delhi was not shy of challenging Beijing on the predatory aspects of its policies, such as the Belt and Road Initiative. It walked a lonely path as even its friends advised that shunning the BRI could have consequences. But New Delhi was successful in making its critique of China's infrastructure plans resonate, as other like-minded nations started to acknowledge the dangers of the BRI. The Indo-Pacific construct took hold internationally through India's insistence that a coherent regional balance of power could be envisioned only when the two oceans were viewed as part of a single, unified maritime space. And India's standing up to China on the border issue in 2020 underscores to the wider region, which has been suffering from the onslaught of Chinese aggression, that giving in to a bullying power is not the only option available.

In this, New Delhi found a partner in Canberra, which was in the process of recalibrating its own China policy. Australia has been one of China's biggest targets in recent years, due to its decision to exclude Huawei from the nation's 5G rollout, its foreign-influence laws and its calls for an inquiry into the Covid-19 pandemic. This has resulted in a sort of kinship with India, which has also been directly targeted by China. India has also taken steps in response to Chinese aggression, including a ban on Chinese apps, disallowing Chinese state-owned companies to invest in infrastructure projects, and keeping Huawei out of India's 5G infrastructure.

Just as without Chinese belligerence a substantive Quad would have remained a distant dream, without India and Australia's proactive stance this grouping would not have been able to move so far so fast.

In October 2020, New Delhi again decided to invite Canberra to join its Malabar naval exercise, along with the navies of Japan and the United States. It repeated the invitation in August 2021, for this year's exercise.

For India, the decision to include Australia marks a major step. New Delhi hopes not only to strengthen its relations with its partners in the Indo-Pacific, but also to send a strong message to Beijing as border tensions mount: India's military partnerships are growing stronger, and Chinese intransigence will make them even more potent. For years, Australia sought to be a party to the exercise, even agreeing to join as an observer in 2017. But India, trying to tread cautiously with China, had been unenthusiastic. By 2020, its calculations had changed. The choice to join forces with like-minded countries no longer seemed radical. By inviting Australia to the Malabar exercise, New Delhi signalled that it might be willing not only to shed its past caution in standing up to Beijing strategically, but also to bear the potential costs of doing so.

As a new geopolitical order takes shape in the Indo-Pacific, India and Australia seem ready to play their part in shaping its contours. But getting to this point required a leap of faith from both New Delhi and Canberra.

The Modi factor

Until 2014, while relations between Australia and India were moving broadly in the right direction, the nations had been unable to overcome their historical baggage. The relationship was marked by relative apathy until Narendra Modi's BJP-led government took the reins.

In September 2014, Australian prime minister Tony Abbott became the first leader to visit Modi after his victory, aside from the leaders of the South Asian Association for Regional Cooperation (SAARC). The two countries signed the Civil Nuclear Cooperation Agreement despite differences in opinion regarding nuclear non-proliferation and disarmament. The next encounter between the fellow leaders happened just two months later, when in November 2014 Modi became the first Indian prime minister to visit Australia in twenty-eight years. He declared that Australia was no longer on the "periphery" of New Delhi's vision "but at the centre of our thought". Modi pledged to work with Canberra at the G20 and regional multilateral forums, to deepen security ties and to conclude a free trade deal. During the visit, the two sides signed the Framework for Security Cooperation, which has guided relations since. The pact included an annual summit, foreign ministers' and defence ministers' meetings, regular maritime exercises and an annual dialogue on maritime security. The momentum was retained even after a change of leadership in Australia, with an annual 2+2 dialogue commencing between their defence and foreign secretaries. This is a diplomatic framework that India shares with only its closest partners, such the United States and Japan.

When in June 2021 Modi and his Australian counterpart, Prime Minister Scott Morrison, held their first virtual meeting, the pair signed a number of significant agreements, including the Mutual Logistics Support Arrangement, allowing each nation to use the other's military bases for logistical support. They also agreed to elevate their ties to a comprehensive strategic partnership, symbolising their commitment to strengthen their engagement. Defence cooperation between the two is gathering pace with the exploration of opportunities for co-production and co-development, as India seeks to invite Australian industry to take advantage of India's liberalised foreign direct investment policies in the defence sector. The two nations have even found common ground on Afghanistan after the withdrawal of American forces and the coming to power of the Taliban, sharing a commitment to ensure that Afghanistan does not once again become a sanctuary for terror groups targeting nations in the region and beyond.

There has also been significant growth in the two countries' political and institutional interactions. After sharing a common platform in the Indian Ocean Rim Association, India and Australia have embraced the emerging trend of minilateralism in the Indo-Pacific. In addition to the Quad, both states are involved in various trilaterals, such as Australia–India–Japan (formed in 2015), Australia–India–France (the first virtual meeting was held in May 2021) and Australia–India–Indonesia (taking shape). These minilaterals provide a platform to deal with non-traditional security issues, and to enhance economic cooperation and initiatives to build resilience in supply chains.

Chinese assertiveness has intensified India–Australia cooperation both economically and politically. The Australian government launched the India Economic Strategy to 2035, while India launched its Australia Economic Strategy in December 2020, facilitating bilateral trade. Australia's exports to India increased from US$10 billion in

2006 to US$14.6 billion in 2016. Most of these goods were coal, minerals, vegetables and cotton. Similarly, India's exports increased from US$1.7 billion to US$6.1 billion in 2016; the commodities included petroleum, jewellery and medications. By 2019, two-way trade and investments accounted for more than US$30 billion each.

The negative image of Australia has started to recover in recent years. By 2020, almost 750,000 people in Australia were overseas-born residents from India. Indian migration to Australia increased from 3991 arrivals between 1941 and 1961 to 398,225 arrivals between 2001 and 2017. Though it was only in 2019 that the number of student visas began to reach the levels they had before the attacks on Indian students, with 96,398 visas issued, in 2020, despite Covid-19 restrictions, Australia hosted more than 91,474 Indian students.

In 2012, the Lowy Institute and the Australia India Institute at the University of Melbourne conducted a survey of 1233 Indian citizens. The results showed "relatively warm feelings" towards Australia, which scored 56 (out of 100), ranking fourth after the United States (62), Singapore (58) and Japan (57). Fifty-one per cent considered Australians to be welcoming while only 26 per cent did not, and 56 per cent felt that Australia would be a good partner to India in the Indian Ocean. A 2021 survey of Indian urban youth conducted by the Observer Research Foundation shows this trust has grown: it indicates that more than 67 per cent of younger Indians trust Australia while only 8 per cent do not. Further, 64 per cent of younger Indians support the strengthening of the Quad and 62 per cent want India to improve relations with Australia within the next ten years. Other studies show similar results. A major shift is under-way as Indians increasingly look to Australia as a partner and as a friend.

Challenges and divergences

Even as the relationship between India and Australia enters a new, more vibrant phase, there remain challenges. For instance, there are concerns in India about Australia's economic dependence on China. In 2020, Australia's trade with China was worth AU$245 billion, or 31 per cent of its total trade – more than that with the next five countries combined. The healthy trade relationship despite growing political differences underscores each country's economic importance to the other. As India recalibrates its economic ties with China, there is a renewed push to strengthen its trade and investment ties with Aus-tralia. How well the two nations succeed remains to be seen.

Negotiations on a free trade deal – the Comprehensive Economic Cooperation Agreement – began as far back as 2011, but it has not yet been finalised despite a 2014 promise from Modi and later com-mitments from both sides. Disagreements over market access for Australian dairy products and meat, as well as Australia's reluctance at opening up services exports, have been major factors in stalling these negotiations. But there are signs that the two nations are now aiming for an early harvest trade pact by the end of 2021. The fact remains that bilateral trade and investment is low, not only compared to China, but also compared to Australia's economic relationships with nations such as South Korea and Japan.

This is tied to the broader China challenge both nations face. For Australia, the challenge relates to its own politics, society and economy, as well as to the security of its wider region. For India, China is a direct military and economic threat on a hotly contested border. India's wider economic engagement in the Indo-Pacific has taken a hit as a result, especially after its rejection of the Regional Comprehensive Economic Partnership, a free trade deal. In November 2020, Australia, China, Japan, South Korea and ten other nations in the Indo-Pacific signed the deal; India did not. A major concern for India was that opening its market up to China would lead to a flood of cheap Chinese goods crowding out Indian-produced products. In contrast, Australia has prioritised its regional trade and economic engagements. New Delhi and Canberra will have to work more closely to integrate their respective approaches to building economic coalitions.

The Indo-Pacific construct has allowed India and Australia to take a fresh look at each other. Australia's broadening of its strategic horizons to include the Indian Ocean, and India's growing footprint in the South Pacific, have made envisioning the Indo-Pacific possible. But whether the two nations can achieve their shared vision in partnership with other like-minded nations is still unclear. ASEAN, for example, is still hesitant to articulate a robust Indo-Pacific vision – a potential problem for Canberra and New Delhi, as both remain keen to keep ASEAN at the heart of their Indo-Pacific vision.

The final – and perhaps the most difficult – challenge is ignorance. For most Indians, Australia is still a faraway land that only comes to the fore during cricket matches. For most Australians, India figures lightly in the political or economic imagination, if at all. The flow of people is almost all in one direction: from India to Australia. Not many Australian tourists go to India, and few Australian MPs or business leaders have ever been to India. Academia, the media and think tanks in both countries have not made a concerted effort to develop sustained knowledge of each other, and although this is beginning to change, progress is slow. Investment in the study of Australia in India and vice versa is still negligible. Not surprisingly, therefore, stereotypes still predominate, and nuance is often absent from our discussions about each other.

As New Delhi and Canberra become more ambitious in articulating their foreign policy priorities, there is a new opportunity to reshape the relationship. Learning about each other –understanding each other's outlook, culture and insecurities – is the surest way to guarantee that this political momentum is not lost. ◼

SEEING CHINA COMING

Behind Keating's pact with Indonesia

James Curran

Paul Keating remembers exactly where he was when he first started thinking about Indonesia. He was on a Sydney suburban train. It was 1965, and he was twenty-one. "I was on a red rattler from Bankstown, in that tunnel going towards St Peter's, and stopped ... where the train was half in the light and half in the darkness, halfway in and out of the tunnel. And I was reading a newspaper article about how Suharto had knocked over the Indonesian Communist Party." It was a crystallising moment. "I was in this railway carriage – and there you have the foundation of the Keating government's foreign policy."

Thirty years later, as prime minister, Keating pulled off what remains one of the most stunning diplomatic coups in Australian strategic history: the signing of a security agreement with Indonesia, the country's largest and most important neighbour. A nation that had struck fear in the Australian imagination throughout much of the Cold War was now tied formally into the arc to our north, a collective strategic bulwark against the unpredictability of an evolving regional environment. The deal not only laid to rest some ghosts of the past; it was also prophetic, foreseeing the potentially destabilising effect of China's rise on the region. In a contested Asia, Australia would be surrounded by allies.

Ultimately, the agreement lasted only until 1999, when it was torn up in the wake of the East Timor crisis. Yet to this day, its formulation – especially the intense secrecy surrounding its negotiation – remains a crucial illustration of a period when a more outward-focused and conceptual Australian foreign policy was in play. It was the capstone of Paul Keating's approach to the region, in which the nation sought to find its security "in Asia, not from Asia". In essence, the 1995 agreement changed Australia's strategic view of Indonesia. In Canberra, Indonesia was no longer seen as a source of expansionism and caprice.

With the release to this author of new archival and policy documents, the story of the 1995 Australia–Indonesia Agreement for Maintaining Security can now be told in new detail. These documents contain briefs from the departments of Prime Minister and Cabinet, Foreign Affairs and Defence, along with records of conversations Keating had with the two emissaries he selected to undertake the secret negotiations, the former chief of the Australian Defence Forces, General Peter Gration, and Keating's principal foreign policy adviser, Allan Gyngell. They also contain accounts of the prime minister's talks with ministers and officials, and, of course, his formal encounters with the Indonesian president. Taken together, they reveal an extraordinary saga of prime ministerial policy-making, as an outdated fear of Indonesia was cast aside in order to deal with a threat that was still nearly two decades into the future.

Through Australian eyes

Australia's relationship with Indonesia has always been different from its relationships with the rest of Asia. This is not just because any attack on Australia must come either through or via Indonesia, but also because the Indonesia relationship marked a rare divergence between Australia and its great and powerful friends – Britain and the United States – during the height of the Cold War.

Canberra and its allies had a fundamental difference of views, especially during the crises over West New Guinea and Indonesia's "Confrontation" of Malaysia throughout the 1950s and 1960s. Sukarno viewed the addition of West New Guinea as the final piece in the creation of his new Indonesian state, but the old Dutch empire, supported by the Menzies government, wanted to retain its last foothold in the region. Ultimately, Australia had to accept that it was not a party to the dispute and acquiesce to the Indonesian demands. The Confrontation episode arose from Sukarno's fear that the creation of the new Malaysian federation was a neo-imperialist plot to encircle Indonesia. As a result of the sabre-rattling, Australian forces joined with British and Malaysian forces in repelling the Indonesians.

On both counts, Australia had to develop its own distinctive policy. Unlike Britain or the United States, it had to live beside its northern neighbour. And, in both cases, the American alliance gave Australia no reason to be complacent about its relationship with Indonesia. Australian politicians and policymakers in this period beat a path to the White House to ask again and again whether the terms of the ANZUS Treaty would apply in the event of a conflict with Jakarta, yet the Kennedy and Johnson administrations were reluctant to dole out the assurances being sought. Experience, then, showed that in a crisis, Australia could not be sure if or to what extent American aid would be forthcoming.

In the 1970s, successive Australian governments also recognised that Indonesia was the key to Australia's long-term acceptance in a region that was breaking free from the rigid bipolarity of the Cold War. They understood that while Australia's conventional military firepower might be superior to Indonesia's, the cost of living in enmity with Jakarta would be tremendous and affect its relations with the whole region. Australia therefore had powerful motives for seeking to prevent disputes with Indonesia from reaching a crisis point. Those motives were evident in Australian responses to Indonesia's actions in East Timor. Labor prime minister Gough Whitlam, a big man who liked big states, believed that East Timor could not be a viable independent nation; it was, as he told parliament, "part of the Indonesian world". Whitlam did not want the question of East Timorese independence to become "another West New Guinea" in the Indonesia–Australia relationship. Thus his government turned a blind eye to, and in some cases even encouraged, the Indonesian annexation of East Timor in 1975.

By later in the decade, Malcolm Fraser could see no advantage in continuing to ignore the reality of Indonesian control. At the beginning of discussions over the Timor Gap Treaty in February 1979, Canberra formally acknowledged Jakarta's sovereignty over East Timor. Subsequent Australian governments continued to hold the view that the East Timorese had a right to decide their own future, which they had "yet to exercise". In informal discussions with Indonesian leaders, the matter was raised. But as Paul Keating put it, none of these governments was "prepared to make the whole of our complex relationship with 210 million people subject to this one issue".

Security in, not from, Asia

If Australia's engagement with Asia was Paul Keating's "magnificent obsession", Indonesia was its lodestar. In April 1992, Keating made Jakarta his first international visit as prime minister. He had told Hawke in their contest for the Labor leadership throughout 1991 that the country was more important than Africa or the Commonwealth, and in an interview with journalist Laurie Oakes in the middle of that year he was clear that strengthening ties with Indonesia would be his foreign policy priority. It was the country "with which we are yet to put the full constellation of foreign policy instruments in place".

Keating was as good as his word, telling an audience in Jakarta during a major speech there in April 1992 that Indonesia was in "the first rank of Australian priorities". He recalls that the reaction to that address was similar to the reception to his Redfern Park Speech:

the more he spoke, the more his Indonesian audience realised that this was different language for an Australian prime minister. As a result of the address, the Indonesian government and business elite, according to then Australian ambassador Allan Taylor, would come to "welcome Australia's participation in the region spiritually and psychologically, as well as physically".

During a private leaders' meeting, Keating also made much of the stability provided by Suharto's New Order government, calling it "one of the most significant and beneficial events in Australia's strategic history". For his part, Suharto made it clear Indonesia had "no territorial designs on its neighbours". Yet he stressed that while wanting closer defence links with Canberra through high-level visits and consultations, joint military exercises, shared training and staff college exchanges, "there should be no bilateral defence pact". Keating did not sidestep the issue of East Timor, telling his host that it was a "great pity for Indonesia since it detracted from what Suharto had achieved", pressing him on the need to find a "basis for long-term reconciliation in the province".

Suharto is reported to have been impressed by his first discussion with Keating, telling his advisers that he admired the Australian's patriotism and praising his readiness to promote an Australia more engaged with its own region.

The groundwork, then, had been laid. There was mutual respect between the two leaders. The question now for Australia was how to channel that connection into a formal agreement: how to make a shared concern for strategic equilibrium overcome Indonesia's outlook on the world, which had traditionally favoured non-alignment. Even if Keating's departmental officials in Canberra could determine this stance to be "anachronistic and sophistry" in a post–Cold War world, they nevertheless had to acknowledge that these were still defining features of Indonesia's international posture and formed the basis of its approach to ASEAN.

A second hurdle would be the Indonesian armed forces (Angkatan Bersenjata Republik Indonesia, ABRI), which had traditionally been "averse to the notion of defence commitments". As the Department of the Prime Minister and Cabinet concluded, "western liberalism is still regarded as a threat, and an agreement with us could be seen to bring it closer".

Keating's grand ambition rarely wavered. But he was about to step into a minefield.

"DFAT teaching egg-sucking"

The challenges in getting the Indonesian political establishment on board was one thing; domestic approval was quite another. The proposal for a defence agreement faced considerable opposition in Canberra. Keating's handwritten annotation on the first substantial briefing on the topic he received from his own department neatly encapsulated the local bureaucratic reaction: "the empire strikes back".

It had fallen to Michael Thawley, then first assistant secretary in the Department of the Prime Minister and Cabinet International

Division, to summarise the criticisms he was hearing from around the bureaucratic traps. They were that an agreement would "be vulnerable to a new regime in Indonesia which would pose a threat to Australia (a Defence worry)", "provide a free kick to an Indonesian government which might want to have a go at us in a bilateral downturn", "link Australia with ABRI's internal security agenda and human rights abuses", and "diminish or blur Australia's commitments to ANZUS and the Five Power Defence Arrangements (FPDA)".

Thawley had relayed what was in essence a two-pronged assault led by the departments of Defence and Foreign Affairs. Their reactions, as Keating's adviser Allan Gyngell warned him at the time, were as much about protecting their own turf as a certain nervousness about Indonesia. Defence minister Robert Ray wanted instead the power to negotiate a memorandum of understanding (MoU) with Jakarta, while foreign minister Gareth Evans, though not opposed to a defence agreement, lent towards a Joint Declaration of Principles (JDP). Not unreasonably, both ministers may have thought that Keating was overreaching. But Keating would not be deterred. He saw an MoU and a JDP as being of token value and insufficient to achieve region-wide strategic objectives. And both ministers, perhaps, underestimated his determination to reach a serious agreement between the two countries.

Keating's private office was one step ahead of the ministers and their sceptical advisers. Gyngell, in a private note to his boss in early June 1994, having read Defence's advice to Robert Ray, underlined that "defence's bottom line is that the idea is premature and the Indonesians won't buy it". He took particular exception to the department's conclu-sion – the brief had been written by Hugh White, then first assistant secretary of international policy in the department – that the purpose of the agreement was merely "symbolic". White judged that "from neither side's point of view is there yet a sufficient basis on which to establish a strategic commitment", citing "Indonesia's ideological aver-sion to formal defence agreements". Gyngell countered that not only would such an agreement be a "strong symbol of fundamental change in the way Australia and Indonesia see each other", but it would also "have practical strategic and secu-rity value for us ... by complicating the planning of any future power contemplating aggressive action in this part of the world". Once again, it was the future, as much as the past, that was in play.

It was unfortunate, he added, "that God had made Australia and Indonesia neighbours"

There was soon some move-ment in Defence's position. According to Thawley, Ray rejected his department's stance of challenging the strategic logic of an agreement, instead stressing that Keating's proposal would constrain Australia's existing defence commitments, worry regional partners and be "unsaleable to the Indonesians". But he still wanted an MoU to cover the existing, and perhaps some future, defence activities.

Evans, on the other hand, was sticking to his idea of a JDP, on the grounds that it would be more acceptable to the Indonesians and would enable more specific defence activities. But the Department of the Prime Minister and Cabinet had already knocked this one on the head, primarily because it would not highlight shared strategic interests and would invite comparisons to the only other such document then in existence, that with Papua New Guinea. The "more substantial it was", Thawley added, "the more difficult it would be to negotiate, because it would cover a wider range of areas and imply a greater sense of shared values and closeness than was the case".

Keating stuck to his proposal in a private meeting with Evans at the end of May. In Evans note of that discussion, the prime minister ticked his approval on each item that Evans brought to the table – with two crucial exceptions.

In red pen, and with a deliberate downstroke of the nib, he simply wrote "NO" next to the proposition that if the government could not secure a formal security agreement, a JDP – with its statement of common strategic interests – would still be "worth considering". Keating believed that officials in DFAT and Defence were too sensitive to concerns that some in Jakarta might think they "may be worse off in reaching too high and failing than not reaching at all". As Evans remarked pithily in that meeting, Indonesian officials might worry that "if [they] get inside the elevator, press the roof button, and it gets stuck, [they] may be cut off from the stairs as well".

But the real point of difference was over the negotiations that lay ahead. Keating bristled at Evans' suggestion that when raising the issue with Suharto, the prime minister would have to be "fully mindful of [the] sensitivities/downside risks" and take them "carefully into account in his presentation". As Keating wrote: "DFAT teaching egg-sucking." After Evans noted that these prime minister–president discussions would take place "on [the] basis of rapid retreat if Suharto negatively inclined", Keating wrote, "NO – but GE thinks I will."

Keating told me that at the time he had most appreciated the fidelity with which ministers Evans and Ray supported the need for confidentiality and sensitivity, and their subsequent support of the agreement itself.

Test of tactics

Secrecy was going to be key, much like for Nixon and Kissinger in their diplomacy leading up to the metamorphosis in US–China policy in the early 1970s. There was a fear that Australian public opinion, especially the vociferous East Timor lobby, might derail the process. There were also other considerations. As Michael Thawley wrote, any risks in getting up a defence agreement with Jakarta could be reduced by "not beginning unless we are reasonably confident of success", by "moving carefully in laying the ground for a negotiation rather than slapping a draft agreement on the table" and by "keeping discussions and then negotiations as discreet as possible": a difficult feat since the opponents of any such agreement in both countries would see advantage in selective leaking.

Settling on the right tactics, then, was "of the utmost importance" to Keating. The usual first step in a treaty negotiation, that the

Australian ambassador in Jakarta give state secretary Moerdiono a letter setting out the broad terms of Australia's agenda, felt too bureaucratic. Similarly, to bring in Indonesian foreign minister Ali Alatas or the head of the Indonesian armed forces, General Feisal Tanjung, would be to court a knockback. The approach had to be at the leadership level. It needed to be based on trust and regard between Suharto and Keating. He wanted to explain to Suharto directly his thinking about the strategic change he saw arising in the region.

Keating was ready. But Evans was due to visit Jakarta before Keating's scheduled meeting with Suharto in late June 1994, and the Department of the Prime Minister and Cabinet understood that he planned to discuss the issue with Alatas. Defence minister Ray was also due to visit after Keating's trip. Keating and his advisers feared that Evans' preference for a JDP and Ray's for an MOU on defence cooperation would cloud Keating's discussions with Suharto – potentially inviting Alatas and ABRI to "be happy to have us pitch our ambitions at a lower level". For the moment, then, discussion of the proposal was to be kept squarely within the walls of the Australian prime minister's office.

On 12 June 1994, Keating flew to Jakarta on the prime minister's RAAF jet. Early the next morning, he drove out from the Australian embassy to the presidential palace. In that crucial meeting, Keating raised with Suharto the possibility of a formal defence arrangement that included some recognition of strategic trust and shared interests. He got a warm reception, if qualified: Suharto agreed that this should be considered further and invited Keating's government to do so and get back to him. But there was to be no public statement. Keating indicated that he would appoint an envoy for this task.

The envoy Keating had in mind was Peter Gration, the former chief of the Australian Defence Forces. Gration had devoted much of his career to building up defence links with Indonesia, and Keating knew he had the confidence of his Indonesian counterparts. In their conversation on his return from Jakarta, Keating provided Gration with a detailed summary of the meeting with Suharto. He pointed out that while the Indonesian president was positive on future defence cooperation – one motivation here was Suharto's resentment towards the United States for cutting off military assistance – he was "cautious about a formal defence agreement, [but] he did not rule it out". As Keating relayed it, Suharto's view was that "if it did not endanger sovereignty and territorial integrity, we should consult in the event of a threat and in building our defence and strategic interests on the basis of our respective national capabilities". Here, then, were the building blocks of an agreement. Suharto, to Keating's relief, also ruled out a JDP.

"You get your chances with history ... your chances at the window of opportunity"

Keating tasked Gration with continuing the dialogue with Moerdiono. He proposed two simultaneous tracks of negotiation. The first was to use existing defence channels to keep building the broader defence relationship. This would give Defence minister Ray the necessary momentum to explore a blueprint for future defence coop-eration. But Keating was adamant that an MOU should "not cut off the option of a wider defence arrangement". In effect, this first track was to prevent Defence's ideas from muddying the larger strategic waters. The second – and the more critical – track was for Gration to explain to Moerdiono "the thinking behind my suggestion of a defence agree-ment and sounding out Indonesian thinking on it".

Keating was careful. He did not want Gration to formally begin negotiations: there was no need to raise the idea of a defence agree-ment with ABRI or other Indonesian ministers or ministries just yet. His task was to gauge their general thinking on defence links to see how best to proceed. As Keating stressed, it was "important that [the] Indonesians understand we're not desperate for this: we have a lot to offer them and the time is right, in my view". Keating had no inten-tion of charging on regardless: there would be no "crash through or crash" mentality – he told Gration straight up that "if they can't cope with it, we may need to leave it, even though the timing with Suharto seems propitious". He knew deep down that his idea might not succeed.

Above all else, Gration's task was to convey to his interlocutors in Jakarta that the proposal stemmed from Keating's own thinking about the "geo-strategic situation which faces us both and which is also behind my approach on APEC". For that reason, Gration was to be accompanied on his first and later visits by Keating adviser Allan Gyngell.

Over the course of the following year, Gyngell and Gration set to work. As Gyngell explained subsequently, "the hard thing" was not "negotiating the language", it was getting Indonesian agreement and ensuring that the discussions were kept secret, away from the prying eyes of respective foreign ministries. There was also an inexplicable nine-month delay in the Indonesian response to the first "non-paper" presented by the Australians, detailing the broad outline of a proposed agreement: Allan Taylor presented it to Moerdiono in October 1994 and there was no response until July the following year. The Australians involved are still puzzled by this long silence, which has never been fully explained.

By the time Keating and Suharto met at the Bali Cliff Resort in mid-September 1995, the agreement was back on the Indonesians' agenda. In their private meeting, Suharto said that he would "pray to God almighty" that the Australian prime minister won the election due for March the following year. For there was work to be done: Indonesia could now "accommodate" the "possibility of an agreement or non-aggression pact" between the two countries. Keating's first response was to iron out the logistics – Gration and Gyngell would again meet with Moerdiono to finalise the text of an agreement. Next Keating, characteristically, invoked the future – he was trying, he said, "to set directions for when he and the President had gone, years from now".

For his part, Moerdiono was sure to stress again, this time to Australian ambassador Allan Taylor, that "Indonesia had no expansionist ambitions", but "he (and by implication the President) accepted that not everyone saw Indonesia that way". It was unfortunate, he added – in a nod to persistent realities – "that God had made Australia and Indonesia neighbours ... But we could not change our geography. We had to live with one another."

By the time Keating met with Suharto next, in Osaka for the November 1995 APEC Economic Leaders Meeting, the text was ready. The agreement – which had treaty status and took much of its language from the ANZUS Treaty – committed the two governments to consult at ministerial level on a regular basis about matters affecting their common security, to consult each other in the case of adverse challenges to either party or to their common security, and, if appropriate, to consider measures to defend their security, which might be taken individually or jointly. As *The Australian*'s editorial concluded at the time, "this treaty can be viewed as an early indication of how the Asia-Pacific power balance will evolve over the next few decades. The 21st century will see a realignment of power, and Indonesia will be one of the countries most involved in that process."

The treaty was signed by the respective foreign ministers, Gareth Evans and Ali Alatas, at a ceremony at the colonial-era Istana Merdeka building in Jakarta on 18 December 1995, witnessed by the two leaders and a pack of media. Keating emphasised to the Australian journalists in attendance that the "weight" of the agreement was symbolised "by the fact that this is the most powerful, in government terms, delegation to have visited a country: the Prime Minister, the Deputy Prime Minister, the Foreign Minister and the Defence Minister".

The agreement attracted international support. Days before its public announcement, Keating had briefed US ambassador to Australia Ed Perkins in Canberra and reassured him that the Indonesia–Australia security agreement would have no effect on the nation's commitments to the US–Australia alliance. Some in Washington were no doubt taken by surprise at Australia's decision to sign a security agreement with Indonesia, but others were enthusiastic about a leader of the non-aligned world entering into a bilateral defence pact with a Western country. And it fitted the pattern of America acknowledging that Australia had special expertise on Indonesia. Keating had succeeded. He had pulled off what the "empire" of doubters in Canberra's bureaucracy had believed to be impossible.

It was as if Keating was setting up for the China challenge to come

Suharto would later confess privately to confidants that the relationship he had with Keating was the closest an Indonesian president had had with any foreign leader since the connection between Sukarno and John F. Kennedy in the early 1960s.

China in mind

What the documents detailing these extraordinary events reveal is just how much this security initiative was about establishing a strong relationship with Indonesia for the future. Keating not only wanted to bury the old fears of Indonesia; he was looking ahead to the possibility of a new threat, in the form of a potentially more aggressive China. He was doing what any prudent leader should do – thinking broadly about the nation's geopolitical future and preparing for any worst-case scenario.

This raises the question of whether fear of China, despite the growing economic, people-to-people and educational links that had sustained the bilateral relationship throughout the 1990s, still lurked close to the surface of Australian regional anxieties. In the 1993 White Paper, Defence officials found "strong grounds for optimism" about the likely benign trajectory of China's growing strategic influence, but they still identified "residual grounds for concern". A year later, Keating was adamant that Australians had "nothing to fear from China", but his rider spoke to the very concerns that would come to animate the strategic debate twenty years later: "Do we want to be in the Chinese orbit ... and feel the pull of gravity of China? No, of course we don't." And in his last major foreign policy speech as prime minister, delivered in Singapore in early 1996, it was as if Keating was setting up for the China challenge to come. He voiced anxiety even as he sought to assuage it in others. China would be a "great uncertainty" in the coming decades, he said, and "the sheer size of its population and economy raise questions for the rest of us about how we deal with it". The answer, in this era, was not to reanimate the Cold War policy of containment: rather, it was to "help China find a place for itself" through APEC and a wider security dialogue.

But this was the public message. It was impolitic, even then, to explicitly finger China as a contingent threat, to voice the kinds of anxieties about Chinese intentions that started to become second nature to Australian political leaders from 2008. While Keating believed – and still does – that China would never make a territorial assault on neighbouring states, Suharto had a different view. The Indonesian leader was suspicious of China, and it was this Keating leveraged to convince his Indonesian counterpart to enter into the agreement.

As Department of the Prime Minister and Cabinet officials argued to Keating, both Indonesia and Australia had "an interest in keeping the United States engaged in the region" and both had "concerns" that US engagement couldn't "be taken for granted". Australian

Keating's proposal was a rare instance of Australian grand strategy in practice

officials agreed that Indonesia would suffer similar consequences to Australia if US nuclear deterrence was not effective and "if Chinese power were not offset". Thus, when Keating spoke to Gration before handing him the negotiator's baton, he stressed that he and Suharto, in their initial meeting, had agreed that "the region was changing fast with many uncertainties: China's growing power, the durability of Japan's strategic client relationship with the US, the outcome on the Korean peninsula, the role of Vietnam". A declaration of mutual strategic trust, he added, would "transform the regional strategic outlook and make the entire region stronger".

It was this future, Keating told Suharto in their September 1995 meeting in Bali, that he "worried about". The final Cabinet submission continued this theme, underlining the reassurance a security arrangement would bring, since "both are in a region undergoing very large and uncertain strategic change". Indeed, it was emphatic that the agreement was a "long-term structure which will consolidate Australia's place in the region, reinforce the stability of our region and help reduce the uncertainties in our future".

Although Australia was not "trying to contain or confront China", the Department of the Prime Minister and Cabinet did include a mock question for Keating in assisting his preparation for press questions. "Prime Minister," it read, "isn't this directed at China?" Evidently, in one sense, it was.

From grand strategy to drift

Keating's proposal was a rare instance of Australian grand strategy in practice. Although "grand strategy" is not a phrase often heard in the diplomatic lexicon of a middle power – it might be said that Australia, in lacking omnipotence, has no claims to omniscience – the story of the Australian–Indonesian security agreement shows a national leader focusing on geopolitical coordinates that were yet to be fully mapped. "You get your chances with history," Keating said in an interview for this article, "your chances at the window of opportunity." The agreement was a way to ensure Australia had "muscular power for a big fight in the archipelago".

History records that the agreement crumbled under the weight of the first crisis it faced: East Timorese independence. On 16 September 1999, Jakarta terminated the treaty after the Australian government suspended all defence contacts with Indonesia. But only the year before, its importance had been acknowledged by then Defence minister Ian McLachlan, who said the agreement had "provided an umbrella under which we can talk more openly ... nobody ever refers to it but it's there".

It would be the basis on which the two countries, under the leadership of John Howard and Susilo Bambang Yudhoyono, would sign the 2006 Lombok Treaty, which established a new pattern for relations based around non-aggression.

Joko Widodo left open the possibility of restoring the Australian–Indonesian security agreement

But Indonesia no longer fits so snugly into Australia's defence and foreign policy framework. The Morrison government's 2020 Defence Strategic Update mentioned it only once. Indeed, in recent years, notwithstanding talks over an economic agreement, the relationship has continued to be one of mutual invisibility. Tony Abbott struggled to fulfil his promise of "more Jakarta, less Geneva", while renewed momentum under Malcolm Turnbull stalled. Part of the explanation for this lies in the dashed Australian expectations of how Indonesia would manage the post-Suharto era. Added to what Indonesian law specialist Tim Lindsey calls "clunky and increasingly illiberal procedural democracy" are contests over

Islamisation, attacks on minority rights and the erosion of free speech. Corruption remains rampant.

Yet Canberra has also tended to either needlessly provoke Jakarta or fail to bring it into its confidence at critical junctures. This, sadly, has been a bipartisan enterprise. There was the Gillard government's crass (and later declared to be unlawful) 2011 ban on live cattle exports, raising prices for Indonesians without consultation on the eve of Ramadan. More recently, there was Prime Minister Scott Morrison's ham-fisted efforts during the 2018 Wentworth by-election, when he signalled his intention to follow the Trump administration's provocative decision to move its embassy in Israel from Tel Aviv to Jerusalem. Morrison ultimately decided against the move, but the damage had been done: the largest Muslim-majority country in the world, which has long expressed its support for the Palestinian cause, witnessed Australia blindly following America and siding with Israel. Morrison is reported to have brushed aside Malcolm Turnbull's warning about a negative reaction in Indonesia, and the move threatened to derail the signing of a free trade agreement between the two countries.

In an interview with Australian journalist James Massola in 2018, Indonesian president Joko Widodo left open the possibility of restoring the Australian–Indonesian security agreement. While renewal is unlikely to happen anytime soon, it could be a way to lock in a new era of strategic trust and cooperation. But that may involve a quite different diplomacy process to the one that Keating and his advisers pursued in 1994–95. Tensions in Asia are only growing. Indonesia has ongoing concerns about Chinese muscle-flexing, and Australia is intensely paranoid over Beijing's ultimate intentions. It is worth pondering just how different the debates in Canberra and Jakarta – particularly over China's rise and the solidity of regional security architecture – might be if that agreement were still in place. ■

THE FIX
Solving Australia's foreign affairs challenges

—

Elizabeth Buchanan on
How to Extend Australia's
Antarctic Influence

"The government should not only approve the Davis
runway quickly ... but must also develop a plan to
use it to Australia's advantage."

THE PROBLEM: Antarctica is the world's final frontier,
a resource-rich territory of immense strategic value. Access to
the continent and its assets have been "frozen" in a geopolitical holding pattern by the Antarctic Treaty System (ATS), which
consists of various treaties that govern environmental and natural resource issues as well as scientific and research activity.
The ATS shelves the question of sovereignty in favour of international cooperation in scientific endeavour. But the ATS is under
pressure. Climate change, resource insecurity and renewed
great-power competition are unveiling weaknesses in the system
and leaving it ripe for manipulation.

Antarctica is no stranger to great-power competition –
following World War II, for example, Germany's and Japan's
Antarctic territorial rights were curtailed as terms of their peace
settlement. The Antarctic Treaty itself was born out of the depths
of Cold War competition. The treaty bans military fortification or
activity (unless in support of science) and the testing of nuclear
weapons or disposal of nuclear waste. Instead, it allows activity
that involves scientific cooperation – even if the parameters of
what that involves are somewhat undefined. Signatories are free
to operate on the continent so long as scientific results are shared
and compliance inspections are unhindered.

Hailed as a magnificent diplomatic coup, the Antarctic Treaty
brought together two enemy camps to forge a peace pact for a far-
off continent. But now great-power competition in Antarctica is
returning – a by-product of China's enhanced polar interest.

Chinese Antarctic activity is a challenge for Australia, but it
is one we facilitated. Canberra supported China's first Antarctic
mission in 1983. In 2015, Canberra and Beijing signed an Antarctic
memorandum of understanding, which essentially rendered
Hobart China's Antarctic gateway of choice. Hobart is one of a
handful of Antarctic "gateway" cities – hubs that provide basing
and logistical support for national Antarctic programs and expe-
ditions. Three of Beijing's four Antarctic bases are located within
the Australian Antarctic Territory (AAT). Yet the AAT (our 42 per
cent claim to the continent) is not widely accepted internationally,

including by our allies the United States. While Australia might view Chinese Antarctic bases as operating on the AAT, Beijing does not recognise these imaginary lines.

China's Antarctic playbook is transparent. It now has an indigenous icebreaker-building capability (a domestic ship-building industry) and diversified Antarctic gateway port relationships. This diversification sees Beijing utilising Chilean and Argentinian Antarctic gateway ports, rather than relying on Hobart's – as per China's memorandum of understanding (MoU) with Australia on Antarctic cooperation. China has increased its "soft-power" footprint in South American Antarctic gateway cities by financing industrial developments and entering into various MoUs on Antarctic cooperation. But the imprecise nature of the ATS (which lacks definitions of even key terms such as 'militarisation', 'conflict', 'war' or 'peace') allows Beijing to interpret it selectively, leveraging the treaty's imprecision to enhance its influence on the continent.

The lines between scientific research and military activity are now more complicated than when the treaty was negotiated in the 1950s. Chinese law also mandates that any civilian technology is made available for military use, which adds to the problem of dual-use technology and activities. Australia is sluggishly waking up to the threat posed by Chinese Antarctic strategy and has started to unravel numerous Sino-Australian scientific research partnerships and funding ties.

THE PROPOSAL: To bolster avenues for international collaboration, and to future-proof the ATS, Australia must build the first paved runway in Antarctica.

A runway has already been proposed, located approximately six kilometres from Australia's Davis Station, in the Vestfold Hills region of East Antarctica. The federal government is undertaking environmental and approval processes; the proposal is still subject to the green light from the federal environment minister, Sussan Ley.

The stated goal is for the runway to be operational by 2040. The government should not only approve the Davis runway quickly, in order to meet that timeframe, but must also develop a plan to use it to Australia's advantage, by transforming it into a project that encourages global research collaboration. Year-round, unfettered access to the continent is a valuable proposition for the international scientific community. International Antarctic programs would also welcome infrastructure that helps to safeguard expeditioners' health and welfare at all times of the year. The Davis runway would strengthen the ATS – by seeing Australia operate valuable infrastructure in Antarctica and allowing it to enhance its Antarctic influence.

Australia first explored the notion of a year-round runway in the 1970s. The ice-free environment of the Vestfold Hills made it a desirable location, and its proximity to the coastline offered further sea-link and wharf support. Australian military surveyors reported the site to have a relatively "benign" climate and predictable weather patterns.

The current proposed runway will be some 2700 metres long, consisting of pre-cast concrete sections. These sections (some 11,000 pavers) will be shipped and assembled on site. The pavers would each measure 5 by 3 metres and are expected to be about 220 millimetres thick. The plan faces strong environmental criticism – some researchers claim that the area around Davis Station features unique geographical features, including fjords and fossil sites, and important wildlife. The runway does come with an unavoidable environmental cost, but it is one Australia is best placed to manage. There is nothing stopping other Antarctic stakeholders from building their own runways should Canberra shelve the Davis proposal. Indeed, plans for a Chinese runway at nearby Zhongshan Station have stalled, with Beijing employing a "wait and see" approach to the Vestfold Hills site. Why build on a sub-par site when the best site might remain vacant? Australia has world-leading environmental standards for Antarctic development – if any nation is going to build a runway, we can do it with the least amount of damage to the natural environment.

The unique landscape – ice-free and rocky – is not found elsewhere on the continent in comparable size. The existing runway infrastructure across Antarctica is rarely year-round, operating largely in the summer months. These runways are often blue ice runways, whose packed ice is a challenge to maintain, let alone utilise (even with ideal weather). As climate change melts the Antarctic icecap, these ice runways are becoming unpredictable. This is where the Davis runway emerges as a viable, safe and necessary international access point to East Antarctica.

WHY IT WILL WORK: Article IV of the ATS protects against any activity being used to substantiate territorial claims, so Canberra won't bolster any existing claim to Antarctica by building the runway. In theory, the case for developing the runway is essentially benign: to support science, to make Australia an Antarctic leader in the logistics space, and to support international Antarctic operations by providing enhanced search-and-rescue or safety support. But in practice, the Davis runway would be a strategic asset for Australia. It would afford Canberra quick, unfettered access to the continent on our southern flank.

More importantly, a runway would help to sustain the ATS, which is Australia's primary (and potentially the only achievable) toehold in Antarctica. Australia relies on the ATS to enshrine our 42 per cent claim in perpetuity and to ensure the continent on our doorstep remains demilitarised. Year-round aviation access would deliver a continuous Australian presence in the AAT – and presence is a precursor to *influence*. Maintaining Australian leadership in the ATS requires sustained influence.

This runway infrastructure would facilitate international research to a degree that Antarctica has not yet seen. Cutting travel time and delays would overhaul global climate research – delivering scientists to the world's longest, uninterrupted climate dataset (Antarctica) and allowing them to rapidly return home to make sense of what they recorded.

This race against climate change is of international interest – it is a security threat that knows no national borders. One option for the Davis runway would be to use it to bolster international collaboration in the same manner as the International Space Station. In this scenario, the runway would need to be internationalised and to become a multinational collaboration, with Canberra taking the lead. This would help reduce Canberra's costs and operational pressures.

To cultivate international cooperation, Australia must forge greater links and collaborative partnerships with neighbouring polar stations owned by India, China and Russia. And we must do it now. International engagement needs to be front and centre in the Australian case for the runway. Discussions between East Antarctic stakeholders should be held to scope out the interest in collaboration – whether this be cost-sharing or assisting in the construction. For instance, access to Russian nuclear-powered icebreakers could ship the pre-cast pavers, or the labour on this mammoth build could be divided between multiple countries. The diplomatic arm of Australian government will need to do the heavy lifting here. After all, the ATS is only as functional as the ties between its signatories.

If the runway is built, Australia will be signalling to other nations that it is permissible to blast Antarctica and lay concrete pavers, yes. Yet the costs are outweighed by the geopolitical realities. Opting to not build the runway will not sway the intent of other ATS members – some of which have already signalled plans to step up their aviation capabilities in East Antarctica. Not only does China have plans to build a runway at Zhongshan Station, but Russia has recently committed to building an aviation base at nearby Bunger Hills. Australia may find that there is even *more* to inspect and keep an eye on in East Antarctica. The East Antarctic aviation race is on, and if Canberra delays, it will be overtaken by China's and Russia's long-term Antarctic visions. An Antarctic runway is a unique asset that offers strategic currency – we must be the nation to build it.

THE RESPONSE: The Australian Antarctic Division declined to comment. The division is part of the Department of Agriculture, Water and the Environment.

Reviews

**China Panic: Australia's
Alternative to Paranoia
and Pandering**
David Brophy
La Trobe University Press

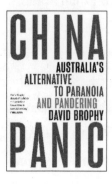

**Red Zone: China's
Challenge and
Australia's Future**
Peter Hartcher
Black Inc.

These two books explore
Australia's contentious
relationship with China,
and they could not be more
different. One lays out
the case for the current hard line
promoted by the government, which
the author sees as justified. The other,
rather politely, seeks an alternative.

Peter Hartcher's *Red Zone*
builds a super-hyperbolic portrait
of China as an all-consuming threat
to the Australian way of life, its
democratic institutions and its
friendship with the United States. In
this depiction, Australia is a fountain
of liberty, China a source of tyranny.
Readers of Hartcher's columns in
The Sydney Morning Herald and *The
Age*, always threaded with the latest
fear-based scenarios dispatched from
Canberra's security apparatus, will be
familiar with the argument.

David Brophy, a senior lecturer
in modern Chinese history at the
University of Sydney, presents
an antidote. In *China Panic*, he
argues, calmly and persuasively,
that Australia is ill-served by this
let's-take-China-on attitude. The
corporate-driven engagement of the
mining industry is not helpful; nor is
the paranoia that seems to motivate
the attitudes of the Coalition

government. It's time, he suggests, for Australia to undo the most egregious of its anti-Beijing policies, framed since 2017 by ASIO. A start could be made by decriminalising the foreign interference laws and modifying the shoddy treatment of Chinese academics. "I don't share the conviction that incurring the wrath of Beijing is in and of itself the hallmark of good policy," Brophy writes.

At the heart of Brophy's book is a common-sense argument about Australia's position towards China and the United States. The extremes – demonising China on the one hand and latching onto the United States on the other – need to be tempered. As much as the threat from Beijing is overplayed, the reliance on Washington is not discussed enough, he argues. This should be seen in the context of China, in the next decade or so, playing the kind of role in the Asian neighbourhood that the United States has taken in the last seven decades. Australia can't afford to treat China as all bad and rely on America as all good.

Many Australians may be surprised to learn that the Australian continent – big, largely empty and out of easy range of China – is about to become a giant aircraft carrier–like base for all manner of American weaponry for use against China.

For the Asia theatre, Australia's distance used to be a liability: too far away for storing weapons and personnel. In the future, hypersonic weapons and AI-empowered autonomous systems that operate swiftly over vast distances will render Australia's distance an advantage. Australia has long played host to Pine Gap and other intelligence-gathering operations. The 2500 US Marines in Darwin, with the numbers likely to rise, are not a mystery. What is little publicised is that in the coming years, Pentagon plans call for Australia to be loaded up with American missiles, naval vessels and war planes. Taken together, the build-up could transform Australia into the most potent American military base outside of Guam.

But there's a disconnect with this military strategy. The majority of Australian adults under the age of thirty view relations with China as more important than those with the United States. Many of them look to China as a lucrative and fascinating place to do business, and few consider it a serious threat to the homeland. Anyway, "none but the most imaginative security hawks can conceive of China ever invading Australia", Brophy writes. Yet these US plans – well known in Washington – are barely debated in Australia. Aside from the security risk, they reinforce the notion of Australia as an "imperial sidekick".

"American military hardware and intelligence facilities on Australian soil, along with Australian ships and fighter jets embedded in US command structures across the Pacific, all but take the question that is most basic to any society – whether or not to go to war – out of Australian hands," Brophy writes. On a depressing note, he adds, "Currently there seems to be no appetite in the Australian parliament for considering the wisdom of the path the country is on, or what it might take to change course." That's because, he infers, hysteria about China as a "uniquely dangerous country" provides a useful lever to whip up a brand of victimhood nationalism.

Instead of these thumping-the-chest policies, Brophy wants Australia to help de-escalate tensions in the region, and work towards demilitarising flashpoints in the South China Sea. It's helpful that

Australia is not fully on board with Washington's freedom-of-navigation exercises. And at least, he writes, Minister for Foreign Affairs Marise Payne declined to be a yes-woman when then US Secretary of State Mike Pompeo suggested Australia should automatically take Washington's side in a conflict over Taiwan. He gives her much lower points for stating that the Pine Gap facilities operate in accordance with Australian and international law. In fact, he correctly points out, Pine Gap supports American extrajudicial drone strikes.

For an outsider peering into Australia, the most extraordinary passage in *China Panic* deals with the delusional reasoning behind the harsh line on China. Australia's tough policies towards China must be considered as a form of international lobbying, Brophy says. Australia's objective is to "rally a US-led response" to China, and to show the world that "engaging with China is profoundly dangerous".

If that is the case, Canberra seriously overestimates its importance in the American debate. No one in Washington or elsewhere in the United States needs distant Australia, no matter how loyal an ally it might be, to cheer them on in the China-bashing era of the Biden administration.

The reader can start with the chapter headings – "Dragon in Your Living Room" and "Daggers in Your Smile" are but two – to grasp the themes of *Red Zone*. Breathlessly, Hartcher recounts that China's spying and hacking in Australia are so rife that it "overwhelms" ASIO's resources. We are supposed to feel sorry for an intelligence agency that requires more money. This desperate situation was caused by Canberra ignoring Beijing's behaviour inside Australia for many years, Hartcher writes. He quotes an American investigative journalist, Zach Dorfman, who wrote that "the number of suspected kidnappings in that country is approaching double digits and includes multiple cases where individuals were beaten or drugged and then dragged into a boat destined for China".

In what is now a well-worn narrative, Hartcher describes how John Garnaut, a former China correspondent for *The Sydney Morning Herald*, came to the rescue, and single-handedly turned around what he considered Australia's lazy attitude towards Beijing. After learning about China's nefarious ways while he was reporting on the mainland, Garnaut came home determined to cut China down to size. He persuaded then prime minister Malcolm Turnbull to tighten the screws against Chinese interference.

Notably, Turnbull barred the Chinese communications company Huawei from operating in Australia, making Australia the first country to do so, and setting a standard followed by many others. Loopholes in investment laws were closed. Actions were taken against activities of the United Front Work Department, a branch of the Chinese Communist Party that tries to influence overseas Chinese.

These were, no doubt, smart moves. But the hype about keeping big, bad China at bay is deleterious to reasonable debate. If one was to take Hartcher's scenarios literally, Australia's attachment to the United States is in danger of being displaced overnight by regiments of Chinese troops landing at the port of Darwin and berthing dockside in Sydney Harbour. Unlikely.

Jane Perlez

**A World Safe for
Democracy: Liberal
Internationalism and the
Crises of Global Order**
G. John Ikenberry
Yale University Press

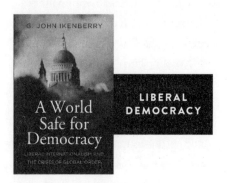

In this compelling book,
G. John Ikenberry has written
a sophisticated defence of
American foreign policy
disguised as a study of "liberal
internationalism". His is the vision
of a world kept safe for a particular
version of free-market liberal politics
in which the United States – for all
its problems – remains, in Madeleine
Albright's phrase, "the indispensable
nation".

Liberal internationalism,
according to Ikenberry, is "an
ongoing project to make the world
safe for democracy". It is hard to
square this with his admission
that liberal internationalism,

pioneered by Woodrow Wilson,
also "has been used to defend
racial and civilizational hierarchy".
Indeed, much of the book reveals a
scholar struggling to accommodate
unpleasant realities to a balance in
favour of American benevolence.

Ikenberry does not deny the
extent to which the Wilsonian view
of the world rested upon a distinction
between "civilised" and other
nations, but he fails to ask whether
Wilson's America, with its enforced
segregation, was in any meaningful
sense a liberal democracy. It appears
that he assumes the meaning of
"democracy" is self-evident. In a world
where all sorts of regimes claim to be
democratic, there is an unconscious
complacency in assuming the
yardstick is the United States, which
The Economist, itself a mouthpiece
of liberal internationalism, identifies
as a "flawed democracy" in its annual
democracy index.

Ikenberry presents a survey of
hegemonic liberal ideas in Britain
and the United States over the past
two centuries, with only cursory
attention to other currents that
have contributed to what we now
call the rules-based international
order. He counterposes liberal
internationalism to realism in

thinking about foreign policy, but in so doing manages to turn the messiness of global affairs into an academic argument. The result is a remarkably bloodless book.

Absence of blood might seem an odd criticism to make of a scholarly work, but what is striking is how little the realities of global inequalities intrude. The Vietnam War, which surely was a major moment in calling into question American hegemony, is barely mentioned. Ikenberry acknowledges that liberalism coexisted with slavery and colonial exploitation, but he seems oblivious to the ways in which the legacies of imperial conquest determine how most of the world views Anglo-American liberalism.

While Ikenberry sees "the formal and informal unravelling of empire and colonialism" as one of "the great dramas of the post-1946 era", he is remarkably vague about the realities. (In the paragraph just quoted, he refers to a radically discriminatory regime in "the Republic of Africa", neither he nor his copy editor having apparently picked up this rather strange term.) His United States lacks an imperial past, overlooking both the war with Mexico in the mid-nineteenth century and the occupation of the Philippines in the twentieth. Ikenberry's respect for Woodrow Wilson, whose presence dominates the historical account, leads him to claim that Wilson's views were central to "the following decades' efforts to discredit empire as a principle of governance" – ignoring the much older history of anti-colonial struggles, most significantly in Latin America and India.

Ikenberry is clearly uneasy with the transition from state-supported social welfare to neoliberal anarchy, but he passes over any analysis of how corporate interests have been significant in shaping liberal internationalist policies. No mention here of US-sponsored coups in Iran, Guatemala or Chile; no allusion to the international trade in armaments; no reference to oil or its role in supporting tyrannies in the Middle East. No invocation, either, of C. Wright Mills and his analysis of the interlocking power elites, nor even of President Eisenhower's warning against the dangers of the "military industrial complex". There is a passing reference to Marx, but a Marxist analysis of *A World Safe for Democracy* would see it as mistaking the ideological justification for dominance for the realities of power.

Ikenberry is sceptical of projects of American interventionism, and is acute in pointing out the dilemma that these can be seen as both the products of liberal internationalism and a repudiation of democratic principles. He discusses this in relation to the unhappy history of the Iraq War, but oddly makes no mention of interventions, for example in Bosnia, that could be better justified by principles of liberal internationalism. It is useful to distinguish, as he does, between defensive and offensive liberalism, and to raise the significance of the evolving norm of the "responsibility to protect". As so often in this book, one wishes for more specific discussion: for example, what lessons can be learnt from the extraordinarily long military presence in Afghanistan – which at various times could be seen as an example of liberal or of realist foreign policy?

At its peak, the US-led Afghan intervention involved troops from thirty-nine countries, surely a classic example of the American-led liberal internationalism that Ikenberry extols. Of course, most of the commitments were small (Luxemburg, Iceland and Slovenia all sent fewer than ten troops), and had most to do with shoring up US support. But that intervention's failure to eliminate fundamentalist terrorists raises key questions about the nature of Western interventions, whether justified in liberal or in realist terms.

The book is most valuable for its detailed discussion of Anglo-American liberal thought and the emergence of liberal-inspired international organisations and civil society movements. But here it is also enormously repetitive; Ikenberry has only one reference to Australia, but it occurs twice, in both cases inaccurately. He attributes the defeat of a proposed amendment to the Versailles Treaty, which sought to make mention of racial equality, to British concern for its interests in Australia, apparently unaware that the independent Australian government was the prime opponent.

For a book premised on the superiority of the liberal international order, *A World Safe for Democracy* offers little that might build the "post-hegemonic consortium of like-minded states" its author sees as the best hope for global peace. Liberal internationalism for Ikenberry is clearly the product of theorists and political leaders in the United States and the United Kingdom, although he recognises that global order depends upon cooperation between very different state regimes. His conclusion highlights the dilemma: he sees the priority as "making liberal democracies safe", while acknowledging that our safety depends on addressing "global warming, the spread of infectious disease, nuclear proliferation, cyber warfare, and terrorism".

The book was clearly written in the shadow of Trump's presidency, though Ikenberry shows admirable restraint in not spending much energy denouncing Trump. But Trump's legacy of contempt for the rule of law and moves to curtail the right to vote lives on. Given the strength of conspiratorial right-wing radicalism in the current Republican Party, some reflection on the United States' weakened authority to promote democracy would have been welcome.

But despite its shortfalls, this is a useful book, because it provides a serious insight into the formative ideas of the "rules-based international order" so beloved by our political leaders. There is much to cherish in the aims, if not the realities, of liberal internationalism. What Ikenberry lacks is the empathy to grasp why this system may not seem so desirable to the majority of the world's population, who see it as supporting a global order that is fundamentally inequitable.

Dennis Altman

A Narrative of Denial: Australia and the Indonesian Violation of East Timor
Peter Job
Melbourne University Press

E ven before a small band of nationalists declared the Republic of Indonesia in 1945, there were big ambitions for the territories that would constitute the new state.

A committee investigating Indonesian independence, set up under Japanese occupation, approved by a two-thirds majority the idea of a "Greater Indonesia" that included not just the lands of the Dutch East Indies, but the colonial territories of Britain, Australia and Portugal. The Japanese vetoed the idea.

Yet it would take decades for Indonesia to finalise its borders and to see the end of colonialism in South-East Asia. This challenge, and how it was perceived and addressed, left an enduring mark on Indonesia's international reputation and on some of its regional relationships.

Indonesia's efforts to remove colonial lodgements on the fringes of the archipelago created a dilemma for neighbours and foreign partners, especially Australia. This was compounded by the polarising politics of the Cold War. For example, there were misgivings in Canberra about the prospect of sharing a border on the island of New Guinea with a potential belligerent at a time when Sukarno was making overtures to both the Soviet Union and China.

Then there was Portuguese Timor: it became the largest barrier to relations between Jakarta and Canberra after Indonesia acted

in 1975–76 to seize and annex the remaining half of an island that had once been divided between Portuguese and Dutch rule.

When the final reckoning for Indonesia's occupation came in 1999, after decades of diplomatic and humanitarian calamity, it plunged relations between Jakarta and Canberra to one of its lowest points.

Peter Job, a one-time East Timor activist and academic, tells the story of Australia's role in the events that led to Indonesia's invasion of Portuguese Timor and the subsequent incorporation of Timor Timur as Jakarta's twenty-seventh province. *A Narrative of Denial* is an account of perfidy and collusion in Canberra in a covert, and eventually overt, Indonesian military and intelligence operation to prevent the emergence of a small, independent state on our doorstep, dominated by what policymakers in both capitals then feared might be a communist regime.

Job relies mainly on official Australian archives to piece together the evidence of Canberra's connivance, although much of relevance has emerged over the years in government documentary releases. He argues that Whitlam and the Department of Foreign Affairs were so convinced that merger with Indonesia was the only viable future for East Timor – economically for it and strategically for us – they were blinded to alternatives. He believes that Whitlam actively encouraged Suharto, both directly and via emissaries, to use whatever measures were deemed necessary to ensure East Timor's incorporation, albeit with some public "obeisance" to self-determination.

As is well known from earlier document releases, Whitlam was unequivocal with Suharto in September 1974 in stating that Portuguese Timor should become part of Indonesia, although he added that this should happen in accord with the "properly expressed wishes of the people of Portuguese Timor". Yet Job suggests that "unofficial" secret policy briefings conducted by the influential Jakarta think tank the Centre for Strategic and International Studies (CSIS) on behalf of senior Indonesian political figures served to entwine Australia in Indonesian planning to the point that Australian politicians and officials effectively became "collaborators and propagandists". By failing to press more vigorously for self-determination and signalling a strong preference for incorporation,

Whitlam and a handful of officials closed off viable alternative means to decolonisation and "facilitated the actions of the hardliners within the Suharto regime". After the dismissal of the Whitlam government in 1975, Malcolm Fraser carried forward this policy of prioritising good relations with Jakarta over "the rights and welfare" of the Timorese people.

These are fair assertions. Given the diplomatic and humanitarian disaster that followed, the policymaking initiated by Whitlam and subsequently embraced by Fraser was even on its own terms an abject failure. Rather than resolve a geopolitical loose end and consolidate relations with a strategically vital neighbour, Australian policy on East Timor – especially in 1974 and 1975 – bequeathed a legacy of bitterness and suspicion on both sides that lingers today.

However, at several points Job does not entertain conflicting accounts and contextual detail that might inconvenience the narrative. One example is a June 1974 meeting in Indonesia between Whitlam's private secretary, Peter Wilenski, and a contact at CSIS, which Job finds spurred Indonesia to contemplate covert operations and military intervention. Wilenski is alleged to have conveyed Whitlam's personal view that East Timor should not be allowed to come under the influence of "another, potentially unfriendly power". The source for this is a memoir by Jusuf Wanandi, one of CSIS's founders. But Job omits an official Australian record in which Wilenski told the Department of Foreign Affairs it was his CSIS contact who "pleaded" with him for Indonesia and Australia to work together towards early incorporation. Wilenski had stressed that the method "must satisfy the principle of self-determination".

In judging international history, it is important to recognise that there are always many complex interactions at play – it is seldom easy to prove cause and effect. The most substantial weakness in Job's account of Australian complicity is the lack of explanation and context for these actions. This is important because it affects the way we perceive Australia's role.

Australian foreign policy under Whitlam was generally enlightened: his government granted diplomatic recognition to the People's Republic of China, pulled troops out of Vietnam, oversaw the independence of Papua New Guinea and restored strong ties with Jakarta after the trauma of Konfrontasi. Whitlam was not an exponent of crude *raison d'état* in international politics. His fears about the stability of a small and economically dependent East Timor were not unreasonable, especially in light of the fate of Portugal's African colonies and the spread of communist regimes in Indochina.

Job largely ignores the real act of malfeasance that gave rise to the East Timor tragedy: Portugal's refusal to countenance an early pathway to decolonisation and invest in capacity-building. According to one US study, after 450 years of Portuguese rule, only two Timorese had graduated from university. That was the true great denial.

Job also overlooks America's role in this sorry tale. As early as 1963, the US State Department circulated a discussion paper canvassing options for encouraging an orderly transfer of sovereignty over East Timor. The seasoned US diplomat Averell Harriman opined that the United States would "have to let the Bung have Timor in 2–3 years at the outside" – a reference to Sukarno, popularly known as Bung (brother) Karno. US intelligence had identified signs that the Indonesian military was preparing to replicate India's 1961 seizure of Portuguese Goa. One US solution was for the Portuguese to "sell or trade" their half of the island to Indonesia. The same pragmatism was evident a decade later.

Job dismisses any influence this pattern of thinking from our key ally might have had on Australian foreign policy in 1974–75 as incidental. He accepts the argument that the United States was "not complicit" in the Indonesian invasion in the "intimate way" Australia was. His sole source for this is some poor scholarship by David Scott, another East Timorese activist keen to finger Australia as the sole culprit. But Washington was well aware of Indonesia's intentions and happy to signal its approval by its silence. A pertinent example is the official transcript of a conversation between Secretary of State Henry Kissinger and a room full of departmental advisers just after Indonesia launched a covert cross-border attack into East Timor in October 1975.

Kissinger: I'm assuming you are really going to keep your mouth shut on this subject?

Adviser: On what?

Kissinger: On this subject, on Indonesia. Also, at the UN ... will you make sure that the US mission doesn't make a statement ...?

Adviser: Aren't they going to call us "murderers"?

[Laughter]

Job has built a case against Australia for aiding and abetting Indonesia's invasion in the manner of a prosecutor, determined to secure a verdict of guilt. There are lessons to be drawn from an appraisal of what was undoubtedly a great failure of foreign policy. One is to appreciate the value of what former foreign minister Gareth Evans termed "good international citizenship" – foreign policy initiatives that are not driven solely by a hard calculation of the national interest. But there were many violations from the United States, Portugal and Indonesia that preceded the tragedy, and these should not be ignored if we are to absorb those lessons fully. After all, even the guilty deserve a fair trial.

Donald Greenlees

Correspondence

"Double Game" by Richard Denniss and Allan Behm

Paul Mitchell

I n their forensic article "Double Game" (AFA12: *Feeling the Heat*), Richard Denniss and Allan Behm highlight Australia's moves to frustrate international action on climate change so as to safeguard our coal- and gas-fired economy. Denniss and Behm document comprehensively the calculated decision Australian governments of both persuasions have made to prioritise short-term profit over diplomatic relationships – betting that these relationships can be repaired once the last tonne of coal has been dug up and shipped out.

While this cavalier approach to diplomatic relations may have worked for Australia in the past (the most egregious example being negotiating an increase in emissions under the Kyoto Protocol, the first global agreement aiming to reduce emissions), this strategy is rapidly running out of steam. Denniss and Behm mention briefly the deep resentment Australia's position on climate change is causing with our neighbours in the Pacific – the region Australia considers its backyard – but it is worth unpacking this further. For it may well be emblematic of a very friendless future for Australia, if moves by the European Union, the United States and other "likeminded" countries and regions towards stronger action at home and the imposition of penalties on laggards come to fruition. As of now, Australia appears to be hurtling towards such a situation with abandon.

For years, Pacific leaders have blunted their criticisms of Australia's climate inaction in order not to upset the self-characterised "big brother" – both primary trading partner and provider of much-needed development assistance. Years of pent-up frustrations came to a head at the 2019 Pacific Islands Forum on the tiny atoll nation of Tuvalu. Leaders could not reach consensus on action to address climate change in the main communiqué and instead penned a separate, less formal statement. Several Pacific leaders were uncharacteristically open in their criticism of Australia's approach to the negotiations and in their perception that Prime Minister Scott Morrison was putting the Australian economy ahead of the lives and welfare of Pacific islanders.

Previously, Australia had sought to deflect Pacific attention on its climate, energy and trade policies by focusing on building resilience to the impacts of climate change in the region. In 2015, then prime minister Malcolm Turnbull kicked this off at the United Nations Climate Change Conference in Paris with a AU$1 billion, five-year commitment, around half of which was targeted at helping vulnerable Pacific nations adapt to the impacts of global heating, such as the increasing intensity of cyclones and rising sea levels. The amount included Australia's $200 million commitment to the Green Climate Fund, the world's largest climate fund; this was sold as a way to help Pacific nations leverage finance from elsewhere and increase the amount of funding available. The remaining $300 million was allocated to "dedicated climate change and disaster resilience programs, and integrating resilience across our Pacific aid investments".

Despite its well-publicised challenges in approving projects and moving funds with speed, the Green Climate Fund has been highly successful in its short life – securing US$20 billion in donor commitments and approving more than 170 projects worth US$9 billion over the last five years. This includes thirteen projects in the Pacific worth over US$1 billion, reaching more than 1.8 million people across nine countries. If, as Australia was so keen for the Pacific to know, its contribution really was about attracting more climate-adaptation finance into our region, it was certainly an unqualified success, and a pretty spectacular return on investment.

But in 2018, Australia declined to contribute further to the Green Climate Fund. Morrison announced on talkback radio that Australia would not "tip money into that big climate fund". This move was resoundingly condemned by Pacific island leaders, Green Climate Fund board members and contributing countries. It no doubt added to the ill feeling at the 2019 Pacific Islands Forum.

The decision was especially galling given Australia had twice co-chaired the fund's board and was credited with helping achieve consensus on funding and policy decisions. As Australia's only non-governmental organisation accredited to the Green Climate Fund, Save the Children Australia understands that the fund is still finding its feet, and this can be frustrating; however, we also understand that it is far, far better to be in the room, working with established mechanisms to deliver much-needed climate change assistance to vulnerable communities around the world, than to be heckling from the sidelines.

Australia's current approach seems to be to do less with less. While it has made further, larger climate finance commitments since 2018 – including a AU$1.5 billion allocation for the 2020–25 period – this funding is largely directed towards "climate-proofing" Australia's aid investments. The funding is welcome. However, in the context of a declining aid program, these funds are being diverted from other critical aid imperatives – Australia is spending less on lifesaving aid in order to say it is meeting international commitments on climate change. For Australia, it's a zero-sum game: since all our climate finance comes from our aid budget, climate finance, as critical as it is, is diverting funding that would otherwise be supporting aid projects in sectors such as health and education. It's the most blatant case of robbing Peter to pay Paul.

It's easy to see why Pacific leaders are fed up with Australia on climate change. It's not just that Australia says one thing about climate in the region and does another. Worse, it pretends to be a friend to the Pacific while actively undermining the region's very existence and offering small amounts of a shrinking aid budget to help offset the effects that our continued burning of coal brings about.

Without a radical shift in domestic policy, and a scale-up in both aid and climate finance, things will only get worse for Australia in the Pacific. The frosty reception Mr Morrison received in Tuvalu is just the beginning of the cold shoulder he will feel around the world as climate action becomes the new normal and the dire consequences of decades of inaction are felt in our region. Given how effectively Australia has managed to pervert climate action through diplomatic manoeuvring, as Denniss and Behm lay bare so thoroughly, imagine what could be achieved for the Pacific if Australia used its influence to catalyse action rather than to prop up dying and dirty industries.

Paul Mitchell is the Principal Climate Change
Advisor at Save the Children.

Nicky Ison

Richard Denniss and Allan Behm's "Double Game" presents a damning account of how Australia has used its diplomatic strength to slow the phasing out of fossil fuels around the world. They show how successive Australian governments have sought to protect, and even increase, exports of coal and gas, and to water down international efforts to drive action on climate change.

The past couple of years, however, have seen a massive shift in the landscape. At home, we saw the devastating evidence of climate change on our doorstep with the bushfires of 2019–20. This was a disaster that climate scientists had long predicted – and warned us about – after analysing the changing frequency, severity and onset of Australia's fire season. Renewable energy sources have emerged as increasingly cost-competitive options to power our homes, transport and industry. Internationally, a more climate-ambitious Biden administration took up residence in the White House, while the European Union pledged to achieve a 55 per cent reduction in its carbon emissions by 2030 and two of our most important trade partners, Japan and South Korea, both committed to net zero by 2050.

Australia now finds itself at a crossroads, with three potential futures.

Climate denial: the first pathway yields to the National Party's agenda to expand fossil fuel exports, against advice from the International Energy Agency. Since reclaiming the leadership of his party, Deputy Prime Minister Barnaby Joyce has said Australia needs to continue thermal coal exports, even though the value of these exports is predicted to fall by $5 billion by 2025–26. Prime Minister Scott Morrison is seemingly willing to shift the Coalition's stance before the United Nations Climate Conference in November, but Joyce has to date refused to sign a net-zero target, citing the lack of a clear plan and unknown costs. If we follow this first pathway, we risk irreparable damage to our credibility and standing among international allies, not to mention financial consequences for Australian businesses and our economy as our trading partners impose punitive measures such as carbon border adjustment mechanisms to level the playing field.

Climate delay: the second potential future is defined by the federal government's claims of a technology-neutral approach, which is meant to support any emissions-reducing technology. However, where they're focusing their efforts is primarily on carbon capture and storage (CCS) and a gas-led recovery. For example, the government recently changed the mandate of the Australian Renewable Energy Agency (ARENA), which was set up in 2012 to improve Australia's "competitiveness of renewable energy technologies", to enable the agency to invest in gas and CCS. The government's actions and rhetoric may appear positive to the untrained observer, but they point to a government that remains determined to prolong Australia's dependence on fossil fuels long into the future. Australia is not alone in pursuing this pathway. Indeed, it is being pushed globally through bilateral agreements, including by a number of Australia's trading partners. However, focusing on speculative technologies such as CCS and fossil hydrogen ignores the technologies that can decarbonise Australia here and now, including solar, wind, batteries and electric vehicles.

Climate action: the third possible future sees Australia taking full advantage of its abundance of natural resources, particularly our world-class solar and wind resources, and securing our position as a renewable export superpower. Transitioning the world to clean, renewable energy in the space of a generation represents trillions of dollars of investments in new technologies, infrastructure, and clean commodities and fuel supplies. The good news is we are well placed to do it. Australia is the world's leading exporter of lithium, but despite realising AU$213 billion in the global markets, only 0.53 per cent (AU$1.13 billion) of this wealth stayed in Australia because we lack onshore processing capabilities. If Australia, as the world's leading exporter of iron ore, was to capture a mere 6.5 per cent of the global green steel market by 2050, it would create more than 25,000 new jobs. Lithium and green steel present two clear opportunities, but there are many more. WWF-Australia's policy paper, "Making

Australia a Renewable Export Powerhouse", lists six types of renewable exports that governments should consider to safeguard a prosperous economic future. With a comprehensive plan to capture our renewable export opportunities and address the manufacture, deployment and export of these technologies, there is far more upside in reshaping Australia as a renewables powerhouse and lessening our dependence on fossil fuels.

Of these three pathways, the first two will leave our economy dependent on fossil fuels and squander the competitive advantage of our exports, which will be increasingly priced out of international markets. Only the third pathway allows us to not only maintain our global position, but also expand our trade into markets where climate action is an increasing priority, such as the European Union. As the EU moves ahead with its Carbon Border Adjustment Mechanism, which will see tariffs imposed on imports from countries with more lax emissions controls, we can either position ourselves to extend our trading relationship or fall further behind.

As Denniss and Behm highlight, Australia's diplomacy carries weight. We can achieve substantial outcomes on the global stage when we have a clear plan and focus our diplomatic resources.

While Australia – through its fossil fuel exports and historical diplomatic manoeuvring – has contributed disproportionately to climate change, our wealth of renewable resources and sectors such as steel and critical minerals mean we can also punch above our weight in contributing climate change solutions.

We can't change our history on climate action, but by leveraging our diplomatic strength, we can help set a positive course for the future. The question is, can we leapfrog from laggard to leader quickly enough?

Nicky Ison is Energy Transition Manager at WWF-Australia and a research associate at the Institute for Sustainable Futures, University of Technology Sydney.

Daniel Wild

Richard Denniss and Allan Behm have made an interesting contribution to the public debate on the international dimensions of Australia's emissions reductions policy. Their central argument, that Australia's foreign policy has been used to support our economy by promoting our fossil fuel sector, is no doubt correct.

Foreign policy starts at home, and it is a key role of government in a democracy to ensure that national interests, as expressed through elections, are promoted and secured through diplomacy. As the authors note, Prime Minister Scott Morrison has stated that "Australia's national interest demands that coal continue to be part of our future energy equation, not just here in Australia, but around the world". This is an entirely unobjectionable statement and reflects the wishes of the Australian people as demonstrated at the 2013 and 2019 federal elections.

It is worth noting the significance of the authors' point that "when emissions reductions from land use, land use change and the forestry sector are excluded, Australia's emissions are rising". On the surface, this is an unremarkable observation, which could be likened to saying that when you exclude the weight someone on a diet has lost, their body mass has not changed.

But reading between the lines, there is a clear implication here: emissions in Australian cities have continued to increase, and regional Australians in the agriculture and farming sectors have been forced to compensate via land use regulations that undermine their property rights and greatly diminish the value of their businesses and landholdings.

A recent research report from the Institute of Public Affairs modelled the economic and social impact of a net-zero emissions target in Australia. That modelling identified that up to 653,600 jobs would be put at risk from a net-zero emissions target, and that those jobs would be overwhelmingly concentrated in regional industries such as agriculture and mining, as well as manufacturing. In fact, close to half of the potential job losses could occur within the agricultural sector.

The research also identified that six of the top ten electorates with the highest number of jobs at risk are represented by members of the Nationals party room (that is, those from the National Party of Australia and from the Nationals wing of the Liberal National Party of Queensland).

These findings are relevant in the context of the authors' astute observation that then Nationals leader Michael McCormack could not recall a single policy area where his party had sided with the interests of farmers over miners. Shortly after the IPA's research was released, Barnaby Joyce returned as leader of the federal National Party and Deputy Prime Minister in large part because of his opposition to a net-zero emissions policy due to its effect on farmers, miners and regional Australians.

Perhaps the most contentious part of the debate about international mandates to reduce emissions is the role of China. The authors only mention China a handful of times, and those mentions are mostly in the context of Australia behaving badly because of our exports of coal to China, which have fuelled its industrial progress and astonishing alleviation of crippling poverty.

However, it is important to recognise that China is the world's single largest carbon emitter, with close to 30 per cent of the global share. Every sixteen days, China produces more carbon emissions than Australia does in an entire year. Under the Paris Agreement, Australia is committed to the deepest per-capita emissions cuts in the developed world, while China is unconstrained.

Any international discourse on emissions policy must have regard for these facts.

Daniel Wild is the Director of Research at the Institute of Public Affairs.

Elizabeth Boulton

Have you ever been at a football match when a player kicks the ball the wrong way? Often the crowds roar, teammates exclaim and the startled player realises what has happened simultaneously. Reading "Double Game" by Richard Denniss and Allan Behm gives one a similar feeling. It's like being in the crowd at the grand final match between humanity and existential threat and realising, with horror, that as the Paris Agreement horn was sounded in 2020 and the match for the Safe Climate Cup began, some Australian players started running the wrong way.

Extinction? Does this sound far-fetched? The year 2020 was also when Australian scientist-philosopher Timothy Ord published his book *The Precipice*, in which he proposes that humanity has a one-in-six chance of going extinct in the twenty-first century. Increasingly, climate risk research (such as on food, water and energy security, extreme weather events or the impacts of a more erratic climate) is morphing into studies of how to survive.

The game has changed. However, what Denniss and Behm's essay highlights is that Australia's strategic posture has not.

The article dispels two common arguments about Australia's climate policy.

First, contrary to the view that Australia's emissions or actions are too small to make a difference, Australia is revealed as some form of coal–gas state – not dissimilar to a narcostate or petrostate in its reliance on a particular resource – which has significant global influence because of its role as a supplier to other countries. Australia's "share of the world's export coal market", Denniss and Behm write, "is larger than Saudi Arabia's share of the world oil market".

Second – and shocking to any Australian who may have been lulled into believing that some sort of steady "technology-led" transition away from fossil fuels was underway – there is a comprehensive and well-resourced strategy to maximise Australian fossil fuel exports and undermine international action on climate change. As Denniss and Behm explain, Australia "is in the middle of an enormous, decades-long project to increase its production and export of iron ore, coal and gas". Using "the full range of diplomatic opportunities available to slow global commitments to net zero", the goal is to "increase coal exports to developing countries in South-East Asia". The generous subsidies and tax concessions for the fossil fuel sector mean that "Australia exports more LNG than Qatar yet collects less than one-fiftieth of the tax", while domestically, a "miners over farmers" dynamic is at play, in which coalmines and gas wells are prioritised over agricultural land use.

The essay does not engage rigorously with the "clean coal" counterarguments espoused by Minister for Resources Keith Pitt, Deputy Prime Minister Barnaby Joyce or Senator Matt Canavan; nor with Minister for Energy Angus Taylor's assurances that the Technology Investment Roadmap will reduce emissions by 29 per cent below 2005 levels by 2030, or similar claims by industry groups. For example, the Minerals Council of Australia website states that expansion of high-efficiency low-emission (HELE) coal technology will reduce coal-related greenhouse gas emissions by 40 per cent, while the Australian Petroleum Production and Exploration Association's CEO, Andrew McConville, wrote in *The Sydney Morning Herald* in August 2021 that Australia's LNG exports "have the potential to lower emissions in LNG-importing countries by about 170 megatonnes of CO_2 equivalents a year by providing an alternative to higher emission fuels". It is tricky to tease truth from spin in such arguments, as it relates to proportion and the cost to achieve small gains. US coal executive Robert Murray, CEO of Murray Energy, said in the years before he died that clean coal is a myth. Similarly, Richie Merzian, director of the climate and energy program at The Australia Institute, dismisses the industry claims of cleaner coal technology. The energy news outlet *Renew Economy* notes there is no modelling or specifics to validate the government's claims of emission reductions in its Roadmap. It may have been helpful if the authors commented on which, if any, of this activity might be legitimate under a responsible draw-down plan.

Many implications arise from the essay, but I will focus on just one: the threat to Australia's security.

While global warming is often described as a threat – existential, catastrophic – the essay depicts an Australian foreign policy in which global climate policy is regarded as the threat, while Australia's fossil fuel sector requires state assistance and protection. This logic did make sense in the twentieth century: for Australia and Western nations in general, access to fossil fuels facilitated national prosperity and was pivotal to military and geopolitical success. Traditionalists will argue that in the context of US–China tensions, this is still the case. But it is not.

What if climate change was framed not solely as an issue of science policy or economic governance, but rather as *the* central threat – what I term a "hyperthreat"? Two immediate ideas arise. One, given that the hyperthreat's destructive power grows in proportion to fossil fuel use, the government is effectively increasing the threat to the nation, amplifying the potential to harm its own territory and population. This belies the state's raison d'être. Two, global military expenditure in 2020 totalled almost US$2 trillion, which reflects expectations of greater conflict over the next decade: the period scientists identify as critical for implementing an effective international response to climate change. Due to its costs and demand for fossil fuels, ardent preparations for war – or actual war – between 2021 and 2030 would likely derail international efforts to act on climate, with irreversible consequences. So the current focus on building up a treasure chest for war could be considered a step towards creating a new mutually assured destruction–type scenario for the world.

While the Nationals' Michael McCormack and Joyce may argue that climate-related concerns about 2050 are too far away to think about now, Denniss and Behm note that similarly long-term security investments are made in defence and space capabilities. However, the more salient point is that, when you consider the nature of the climate system, the physics of prior emissions, current allowances for future emissions, the ten- to twenty-year time lag between emissions release and their warming impact, and the time required to build and establish zero-emission pathways, now is the critical time for decision-making. As we saw with the delayed decision to evacuate Afghan staff who helped Australian military forces, waiting to see how a situation evolves *is* a decision, because it closes off the chance to act while it is still possible.

Australia's threat posture is incongruent. It suffers from strategic lockjaw, oriented to a pre-climate security era that does not appreciate that the nature of threat and destruction has changed fundamentally. Thinking of climate change as a hyperthreat alerts us to a new form and scale of harm-doing, killing and destruction, which requires a completely new strategy.

What to do about it? Internationally, Australia's diplomatic assets would ideally work towards establishing a regional Climate Emergency Peace Treaty over the 2021–30 period. This would allow all countries to focus on preparing to counter and contain the hyperthreat. Critically, this would include resetting the Australia–China relationship. As other authors in *Feeling the Heat* suggest, the opportunities in eco innovation are immense, yet require skill and expertise to realise. Prospects for partnerships with China could exist in electric vehicle manufacturing, renewable energy, recycling, drought-tolerant agriculture, water efficiency, regional disaster response and meteorology. Conducting a multilateral planning activity on how to "contain the hyperthreat" in the Indo-Pacific could be a bold way to kickstart a new era of collaboration.

Domestically, aside from shifting federal support to the hungry new players in the renewables sector, the phenomenal engineering and technical might of Australia's old hands in the resources industry must be harnessed and directed towards the right goal – a rapid path to zero emissions. With all players running the same way, there is a possibility humanity could recover lost ground and rein in some of the hyperthreat's destructive power. This is the government's key challenge.

Elizabeth Boulton has a PhD in climate and environmental change
from the Australian National University.

Richard Denniss responds

"**A** leaked email has revealed how Australia pressured the UK to drop binding commitments to the Paris climate change agreement from the UK–Australian trade deal. *Sky News* reports that the Morrison Government insisted that 'a reference to Paris Agreement temperature goals' be removed from the text of the trade deal."

I read those sentences as I sat down to write this response to the correspondence concerning Allan Behm's and my essay "Double Game", and I thought, *Somehow I don't think our thesis will be undermined by the facts as they emerge in the decades ahead.*

While all of the respondents provided thoughtful and insightful comments, I confess to a favourite. Institute of Public Affairs Director of Research Daniel Wild opens his correspondence with the observation that our "central argument, that Australia's foreign policy has been used to support our economy by promoting our fossil fuel sector, is no doubt correct". Given how defensive the IPA usually is of the subsidies, cheap loans and lax regulations provided by successive Australian governments to the fossil fuel industry, such a generous and unequivocal acceptance of our central premise is heartening.

It is easy for Australian governments to tell their citizens that they are serious about climate change while doing little if anything to actually address it, but in diplomatic settings, what matters is not what governments tell their voters about priorities, but what they push for behind closed doors. As the evidence in our essay shows, the Australian government has spent decades slowing global efforts to reduce greenhouse gas emissions in order to "make room" for the expansion of Australian fossil fuel exports. The IPA's support for such a use of Australia's diplomatic power is as revealing as the government's leveraging of the diplomatic community itself.

Elizabeth Boulton, on the other hand, approaches the conclusion of our essay from quite a different, but illuminating, perspective. She defines the strategic threat to Australia posed by climate change as a "hyperthreat" that should result in a significant recasting not only of Australia's economic and diplomatic strategy, but also of our assessment of future military threats as well.

The Australian government's failure to confront the challenges and opportunities caused by climate change are also canvassed by Nicky Ison, who suggests that Australia must choose between denial, delay or climate action. While she makes the case for the benefits of leaping from "laggard to leader", including through recasting our diplomatic efforts, somehow I suspect that she lacks optimism that such a shift will eventuate in the short term – a (possible) pessimism that the recent reporting of our free trade agreement negotiations would seem to validate.

Finally, Paul Mitchell provides clear examples of how decades of diplomatic protection for the fossil fuel industry, which complements the financial protection provided through the Australian federal budget, have both harmed our relations with the Pacific and impeded the ability of international bodies such as the Green Climate Fund to help lift billions of people out of energy poverty while reducing the world's reliance on fossil fuels. He concludes by asking us to imagine a different path: "Given how effectively Australia has managed to pervert climate action through diplomatic manoeuvring ... imagine what could be achieved for the Pacific if Australia used its influence to catalyse action rather than to prop up dying and dirty industries."

Let's pause on that line. Imagine if we did. Imagine if Australia abandoned not just its financial support for the fossil fuel industry (as it has already, promised its G20 allies it will) but also its diplomatic support for the industry. Imagine if Australia went to the United Nations Climate Change Conference in Glasgow in November 2021 with significantly more ambitious commitments to reduce emissions and a new desire to subsidise renewable energy in the Pacific, rather than new coal mines and gas wells in Australia. How transformative to our relationship with the Pacific that would be – and how transformative to our relationship with the Biden administration, at a time when Australia craves the United States' continued involvement in the Pacific.

It is easy to see why groups such as the IPA are so strongly in favour of Australia's diplomatic support for the fossil fuel industry – they simply understand how valuable that support is.

My thanks to all of our correspondents for their thoughtful contributions. The louder the debate about the role of diplomatic protection for Australia's fossil fuel industry, the sooner the situation is likely to change.

But while Australians come to realise how expensive our financial support for the fossil fuel industry is (the Australia Institute estimates it at over AU$10 billion per year), the only way to discover the significant costs of our diplomatic support for the fossil fuel industry would be to abandon it. Likely nothing would transform our relationship with the Pacific, and our major allies, faster. But after decades of waiting, I won't hold my breath.

Richard Denniss is chief economist at the Australia Institute.

Subscribe to Australian Foreign Affairs & save up to 28% on the cover price.

Enjoy free home delivery of the print edition and full digital as well as ebook access to the journal via the Australian Foreign Affairs website, iPad, iPhone and Android apps.

Forthcoming issue:
The Taiwan Choice
(February 2022)

Never miss an issue. Subscribe and save.

☐ **1 year auto-renewing print and digital subscription** (3 issues) $49.99 within Australia. Outside Australia $79.99*.

☐ **1 year print and digital subscription** (3 issues) $59.99 within Australia. Outside Australia $99.99.

☐ **1 year auto-renewing digital subscription** (3 issues) $29.99.*

☐ **2 year print and digital subscription** (6 issues) $114.99 within Australia.

☐ Tick here to commence subscription with the current issue.

Give an inspired gift. Subscribe a friend.

☐ **1 year print and digital gift subscription** (3 issues) $59.99 within Australia. Outside Australia $99.99.

☐ **1 year digital-only gift subscription** (3 issues) $29.99.

☐ **2 year print and digital gift subscription** (6 issues) $114.99 within Australia.

☐ Tick here to commence subscription with the current issue.

ALL PRICES INCLUDE GST, POSTAGE AND HANDLING.

*Your subscription will automatically renew until you notify us to stop. Prior to the end of your subscription period, we will send you a reminder notice.

Please turn over for subscription order form, or subscribe online at **australianforeignaffairs.com**
Alternatively, call 1800 077 514 or +61 3 9486 0288 or email **subscribe@australianforeignaffairs.com**

Back Issues

ALL PRICES INCLUDE GST, POSTAGE AND HANDLING.

- [ ] **AFA1** ($15.99)
  The Big Picture
- [ ] **AFA2** ($15.99)
  Trump in Asia
- [ ] **AFA3** ($15.99)
  Australia & Indonesia
- [ ] **AFA4** ($15.99)
  Defending Australia
- [ ] **AFA5** ($15.99)
  Are We Asian Yet?
- [ ] **AFA6** ($15.99)
  Our Sphere of Influence
- [ ] **AFA7** ($15.99)
  China Dependence
- [ ] **AFA8** ($15.99)
  Can We Trust America?
- [ ] **AFA9** ($15.99)
  Spy vs Spy
- [ ] **AFA10** ($15.99)
  Friends, Allies and Enemies
- [ ] **AFA11** ($22.99)
  The March of Autocracy
- [ ] **AFA12** ($22.99)
  Feeling the Heat

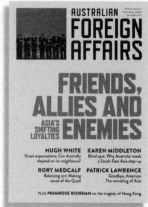

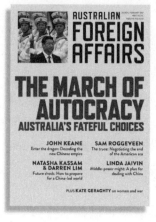

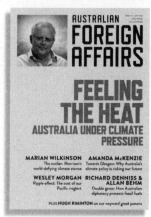

PAYMENT DETAILS I enclose a cheque/money order made out to Schwartz Books Pty Ltd. Or please debit my credit card (MasterCard, Visa or Amex accepted).

CARD NO.

EXPIRY DATE   /   CCV   AMOUNT $

CARDHOLDER'S NAME

SIGNATURE

NAME

ADDRESS

EMAIL   PHONE

Post or fax this form to: Reply Paid 90094, Carlton VIC 3053 **Freecall:** 1800 077 514 **or** +61 3 9486 0288
Fax: (03) 9011 6106 **Email:** subscribe@australianforeignaffairs.com **Website:** australianforeignaffairs.com
Subscribe online at australianforeignaffairs.com/subscribe (please do not send electronic scans of this form)

A FREE PODCAST ABOUT FOREIGN AFFAIRS IN AUSTRALIA AND THE ASIA-PACIFIC

"Why would a career politician camouflage as working-class? For power."

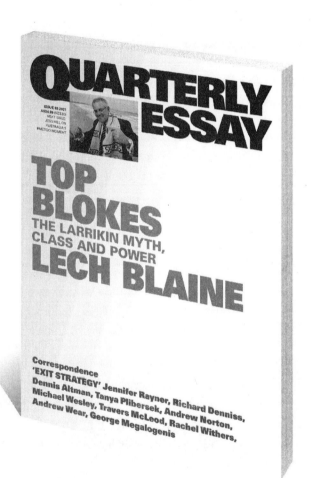

The Back Page

MINILATERALISM

What is it: Flexible alignments between a small number of countries. The G5, G7, Quad (Australia, United States, India and Japan) and so-called "climate clubs" with non-binding, non-Kyoto targets are examples.

How small is small: William T. Tow (professor, Australian National University) is among those who say minilateral agreements usually involve three or four nations. However, agreements between as few as two states (like the Franco–British Lancaster House Treaties) or as many as twenty (like the G20) have also been described as minilateral.

Mini or multi: Minilateralism can be defined in contrast to multilateralism. According to Stewart M. Patrick (fellow, Council on Foreign Relations), it is "voluntary rather than legally binding; disaggregated rather than comprehensive; trans-governmental rather than just intergovernmental; regional rather than global; multi-level and multi-stakeholder rather than state-centric; and 'bottom-up' rather than 'top-down'".

Where did it come from: Minilateralism has been much-discussed in the aftermath of Brexit and Trump, amid concerns about rising unilateralism, but a longer-term decay in multilateral institutions may be responsible. As Moisés Naím (former editor in chief, *Foreign Policy*) put it, "since the early 1990s, the need for effective multicountry collaboration has soared, but at the same time multilateral talks have inevitably failed".

Does it work: It depends. Robert Falkner (associate professor, London School of Economics and Political Science) is sceptical, believing it is "unlikely to overcome the structural barriers to a comprehensive and ambitious international climate agreement". Nevertheless, some minilateralism lasts: the ANZUS Treaty, struck between three nations, just turned seventy.